MVFOL

¡FLAM

Text by Gwynne Edwards

Photographs by Ken Haas

ENCO!

Thames & Hudson

Color photographs © 2000 Ken Haas
Text © 2000 Thames & Hudson Ltd, London

First published in hardcover in the United States
of America in 2000 by Thames & Hudson Inc.,
500 Fifth Avenue, New York, New York 10110

Library of Congress Catalog Card Number 00-101121
ISBN 0-500-51018-0

Printed in Hong Kong by Toppan Printing Co.

CONTENTS

FOREWORD

If I know some twenty distinct definitions of flamenco, it is because I have asked that many aficionados to express the meaning of the art they love. I could have enjoyed thirty definitions if I had bothered to ask ten others.

What, then, constitutes 'real' flamenco rather than the distilled or diluted? Is flamenco purely an expression of the gypsy experience or was it formed by other Andalusian influences, such as the music of the urban proletariat or the miners of Asturias as well? Does it include the rich Sevillano or is that sensual dance a tradition apart? Is flamenco robust, as it fuses in places with jazz or pop, or is it in decline, never to be as good as it was in 'the old days'? The scholar Timothy Mitchell has commented that the story of flamenco was never written by historians, only aficionados, and it has made for a partisan telling.

In this explosive mix there is a dollop of what Spaniards call 'patriotismo', the chauvinism that prizes what was produced in one's home city or province over the second-rate stuff issued elsewhere. While the Spaniards have a special word for it, it is not unique to them; I've certainly experienced it in the opera houses of Italy or among the gourmets of China. As to the contribution of the gypsies, a culture fated to be either romanticized or reviled by outsiders, I think it is safe to say that they are not the entire story of flamenco. But if they were removed from the equation, flamenco would not exist in any form that we would recognize today. To imagine flamenco without them would be to imagine jazz without African-Americans.

I do not seek to document flamenco in these photographs, or to catalogue what is worthy or distinguished in the art. My images are merely impressions of the feelings I sensed in my exposure to this unique Andalusian outpouring. Their aim is to convey the edgy rhythms and heart-rending sadness, the fluid beauty, the sense of a shared past and haze of sacramental wine, which swirl around the chimera called 'flamenco'.

KEN HAAS

26 January 2000

CHAPTER *1*
The origins and the art of flamenco

THE SETTING: a *tablao* or flamenco night-club somewhere on the Costa del Sol. A dark-haired, dark-skinned young woman in a tight polka-dot dress with a flamenco train hammers out with her heels a fast and exciting rhythm. A seated guitarist accompanies her, and the other dancers and singers who make up the group punctuate the dance with their clapping while shouting their encouragement. However appealing this image may be, it is one-dimensional: the art of flamenco derives from complex social, cultural and historical processes from the fifteenth century to the present.

The word flamenco, which applies to the song, the dance and the guitar, did not come into use until the nineteenth century, and there are various theories regarding its meaning and origin. One suggestion is that before they arrived in Spain, a large contingent of gypsies passed through Flanders and therefore came to be known as flamencos, which is the Spanish word for 'Flemings'. It is an opinion discredited by the fact that this event occurred four centuries before the word came to be applied to the gypsies. Another suggestion, even more unlikely, is that, since flamenco also means 'flamingo', it was used to describe the flamingo-like posture the gypsy dancer frequently adopts. A third possibility, rather more feasible, is that flamenco derives from two Arabic words, 'felag' and 'mengu', which together mean 'fugitive peasant', and that, having initially been applied to persecuted fugitives of Arabic origin, it later came to embrace all such people, inclufing the gypsies. The most likely theory, however, is that flamenco is a derivative of 'flamma', meaning 'flame', and that it was used to describe the fiery and flashy gypsy character and, by extension, their music and dance.

The first recorded reference to the gypsies in Spain dates from 1447, when they were reported to be in Barcelona, though it seems likely that another group had arrived in the south of Spain

OPPOSITE,
A flamenco singer of the nineteenth century. Etching by Luis Arajo, 1884

A caravan of gypsies, in an etching by Jacques Caillot, *c.* 1621

Gustave Doré was fascinated by gypsies and their dances. In this illustration to a book about Spain in 1875, he shows a gypsy woman dancing the 'Zorongo'.

well before this date, having originally migrated from India to different parts of Europe, Africa and Asia around AD 1000. In any case, it was in the south of Spain, with its attractive terrain and climate, that in the course of time the gypsies as a whole settled, and the name *gitanos*, which had at first been applied by Spaniards only to those gypsies who had entered Andalusia from Egypt – *gitanos* being a distortion of *egiptanos* ('Egyptians') – came to be used to describe all of them.

From the moment of their arrival in Spain, as in the rest of Europe, the gypsies acquired a bad reputation. Their vagabond existence caused the local people to regard them with fear and suspicion; they were considered to be thieves, thugs, and even murderers. They were associated with witchcraft, especially the evil eye, with fortune telling and the dark secrets of herbal remedies. Their swarthy appearance, the wearing of rings on their ears, and their strange language added to their notoriety; and their music and dancing, often taking place around camp fires at night, led to the belief that they were involved in demonic rituals. George Borrow, writing in the nineteenth century of the history of the gypsies in Spain, drew the following conclusion:

> ...formidable in point of number, their presence was an evil
> curse in whatever quarter they directed their steps... mules and
> horses were stolen, carried away to distant fairs, and there disposed
> of ... flocks of sheep and goats were laid under requisition to assuage
> the hungry cravings of these thievish Cormorants.

Borrow's hostile view clearly encapsulates the way the gypsies were still regarded over the centuries by equally narrow-minded Spaniards.

Between 1499 and 1783 the gypsies became the object of laws introduced by successive Spanish monarchs to oblige them to abandon their nomadic ways. The Catholic Kings, Ferdinand and Isabella, in 1499; Philip II in the late sixteenth century; Philip IV in 1663; and Charles II subsequently, all sought to curb the freedom of the gypsies and to punish their misdemeanours by means of measures which, among other things, forced them to settle in one place and to engage in respectable work. Failure to comply often resulted in condemnation to the galleys for a period of six years. Only in the last quarter of the eighteenth century, during the reign of Charles III, were the gypsies treated more sympathetically.

The effect of such oppression over a long period of time was, naturally enough, that many of the gypsies settled down and that gypsy districts, known as *gitanerías*, sprang up in many towns and cities such as Cádiz, El Puerto de Santa María, Granada and Seville. Borrow's account of these communities, though exaggerated, describes their poverty, the professions or trades taken up by the men – blacksmiths and horse-handlers – and significantly the fiery nature and the dancing of the gypsy women which, in the evenings, attracted the attention of young and dissolute aristocrats:

> The gypsy women and girls were the principal attractions to these visitors;... there can be no doubt...that they are capable of exciting passion of the most ardent description, particularly in the bosoms of those who are not of their race... No females in the world can be more licentious in word and gesture, in dance and song, than the Gitanes.

Borrow's tales of the gypsies' more settled way of life and of what is clearly *flamenco* performance could easily have been true of the gypsy district of Granada, the Sacromonte, and of Triana in Seville, one of the oldest gypsy communities in Spain.

It seems clear too that, as time passed, the group of people known as the gypsies came to incorporate other elements, some of them ethnic, and that the word *gitanos* began to be used rather loosely to refer to fellow travellers who included beggars, escaped criminals, runaway slaves, and, in particular, Jews and *Moriscos* who chose to disappear into and be absorbed by gypsy communities. If, as we have seen, the gypsies were persecuted from the end of the fifteenth century onwards for their vagabond existence, the fate of the Jews and the *Moriscos* was, for religious reasons, even harsher. Forced to accept the Christian faith from as early as 1391, converted Jews or *conversos*, as they were called, were either forced out of Spain, deprived of their living, or burnt at the stake, while the treatment of unconverted Jews was consistently brutal. As for the *Moriscos*, or converted Moors, systematic repression from 1492 – the year which marked the end of more than seven hundred years of Moorish domination of Spain – involved at different times exile, abandonment of their traditional ways, torture, expulsion and death. Despite resistance such as that of the *Moriscos* of the Alpujarra mountains in 1568, when 30,000 rebels fought the royal armies for three years, it is estimated that by

'The little dancing girl' is a detail from a fifteenth-century Belgian tapestry depicting gypsy life.

Travelling musicians,
by Doré

1614 some 300,000 *Moriscos* had left the country. Those who chose to remain clearly sought refuge among people and in communities which would have been sympathetic to their plight and where, they believed, they would be safe from detection – in short, among the gypsies. The latter, after all, claimed to be Christians and were not persecuted for religious reasons. Jews and *Moriscos* who disappeared into such communities could not only conceal their identity by changing their name but also continue to practise their own religion in secret. In addition, an element of safety was afforded by the fact that the gypsies enjoyed the protection of those aristocrats who regularly frequented their communities in search of entertainment, drink and sex. Proof that many *Moriscos* were indeed absorbed in this way lies in the fact that, twenty-five years after their expulsion from Spain, the gypsies suddenly proved to be experts at something with which they had never been associated – working the land, a particular skill of the *Moriscos*.

The point needs to be made too that during the sixteenth and seventeenth centuries – the pinnacle of Spain's imperial power the size, importance, wealth and population of many towns and cities in south-western Andalusia increased considerably, not least as a direct result of trade with South America. The population of Seville rose, for example, from 95,000 in the middle of the sixteenth century to 150,000 by 1640. There, as well as in other towns, the number of beggars, petty criminals, and slaves grew considerably. In the middle of the sixteenth century El Puerto de Santa María became the headquarters of the Royal Galleys, to which many petty criminals were condemned, and many *Moriscos*, in spite of the expulsion order, worked in the fishing industries of Cádiz. In short, as Timothy Mitchell has pointed out, this particular area of south-western Andalusia, which became the cradle of *flamenco*, contained a number of marginalized and disadvantaged groups.

Here the gypsies were prominent but Jews, *Moriscos*, slaves, beggars, labourers and petty criminals were also present: they, like the gypsies, had their own communities. Persecution by those in authority linked all these groups who shared a common sense of injury and trauma, leading them to seek relief and escape in some form of self-expression.

Singing was one way of achieving this, a single singer, a *cantaor*, expressing not only his own sense of hurt but also that of his listening audience, so that the latter was both observer and, in a key sense, participant. This may well have been the context in which flamenco song came to the fore, described at

this stage by the word *gitano* rather than *flamenco*. The release of pent-up·
emotion experienced by the group as a whole but channelled through a single
singer was likely to have been encouraged by the fact that their meeting places
were inns and taverns, with liberal amounts of alcohol freeing them from any
sense of inhibition: What songs were sung on such occasions and how did
they develop into the style first known as *gitano* and later *flamenco*?

Well before the sixteenth century there existed throughout Spain a rich
ballad tradition, a treasure-house of short poems or *romances* which, before the
invention of printing, were transmitted orally from person to person and generation to generation. The ballads dealt with a wide range of themes and
subjects, from the enmity between noble families to emotions between lovers
and the anguish of particular individuals. Accompanied by a guitar or guitar-
like instrument, the ballads were sung by many different kinds of people:
blind men and women trying to keep body and soul together; pedlars selling
their wares; and, of course, the gypsies, many of whom continued to travel the
length and breadth of Spain singing for money, in spite of the laws introduced

A drawing by Goya
of a blind couple
singing, based on an
Andalusian journey he
took around 1805

'Guitar Player', a popular Spanish woodcut of the nineteenth century

A woodcut of 1852 illustrating a collection of Andalusian popular songs

OPPOSITE, An illustration by Doré of gypsies dancing in Seville, and an illustration of 1847 from a book devoted to scenes from Andalusia

against them. Given the fact that the ballads were sung throughout Spain by a variety of individuals, why was it, then, that the ballads were transformed into flamenco song in Andalusia when such a transformation did not occur elsewhere?

One explanation is that the gypsies of Andalusia developed and transformed the ballads in their own way, fragmenting the longer poems into mainly three- or four-line songs known as *coplas*, colouring them with their own characteristic language – a hybrid of Romani and Andalusian-pronounced Castilian – and adapting them to their style of singing. This development, moreover, is likely to have taken place in those more settled communities alluded to earlier where a strong sense of communal anguish clearly existed. In the seventeenth and eighteenth centuries Triana, across the river from the centre of Seville, would have been precisely that kind of community – largely inhabited by gypsies but a refuge too for many other unfortunates, all of whom felt both the sting of injustice and aggression towards their oppressors.

In adapting the traditional ballads to their own ends, it is highly likely that such groups would have sung them not in a gentle, lyrical style, as was the case with the ballads in other parts of Spain, but in a rough, raw manner appropriate to their feelings of rejection and hostility – in short, a style which acquired the name of the people who employed it: *cante gitano* and subsequently *cante flamenco*. And if this raucous and flashy dramatic style was initially not the creation of the gypsies alone but of that mixture of marginalized individuals who were loosely described as *gitanos*, the likelihood is that the gypsies themselves proved to be the most adept at 'marketing' that style. Not only were they experienced performers in singing for money, they were also the largest outsider group in Andalusia, highly conscious of their marginalization over many centuries. By the time specific evidence existed of what we now call flamenco – the 1770s – the gypsies had largely appropriated for themselves this style of singing.

In the evolution of flamenco in the eighteenth century, the role played by the aristocracy also proved important. Not only did aristocrats visit gypsy communities in search of entertainment; in many cases they adopted gypsy dress, manners and speech, probably as a reaction against aristocratic refinement and sophistication. And most important, they sponsored the so-called *juerga*, an organized party or gathering in taverns and similar establishments where they would be entertained by gypsy singing and dancing to the accompaniment of a plentiful supply of alcohol. The Spanish writer, José Cadalso, provided a vivid account of such an occasion when, around 1773, he was travelling to Cádiz:

...we arrived at the estate. He [tío Gregorio] introduced me to those present, various friends or relatives of his of the same age, class and upbringing... he announced the name and described the qualities of each gypsy woman, beat out the rhythm with his hands when one of his excited protectors [i.e. an aristocrat] danced, and drank their health with a half jug of wine... I will only say that the smoke of the cigars, tío Gregorio's shouting and clapping, the sound of all those voices, the noise of castanets, the discordant guitar, the raised voices of the gypsy women over which would play the *polo* for Preciosilla to dance, the barking of the dogs and the out-of-tune singing, stopped me sleeping a wink...

Basically, the *juerga* has not changed to this day, for twentieth-century accounts attest to the presence of gypsies and aristocrats, the consumption of large amounts of alcohol, and the highly charged emotional nature of the occasion.

The Andalusian nobility also contributed to the development of the flamenco form known as the *saeta* ('arrow': one that pierces the heart), a song of lamentation dedicated to the images of the Virgin Mary and the crucified Christ as they are carried through the streets during Holy Week. Originally, the *cofradías* or brotherhoods, created in the seventeenth century to promote charitable work, and in which the aristocracy had considerable influence, would have the procession of penitents stop in front of a prison so that the inmates could sing a *saeta* and thus release their pent-up feelings of guilt. Subsequently, the *saeta*, no longer sung by prisoners but by professional singers, *saeteros*, who would appear on a balcony as the procession passed by, became an established part of the Holy Week processions and continues to this day in cities, towns and villages alike.

More precise information about the evolution of flamenco became available during the first half of the nineteenth century. At this stage, flamenco song in its

A portrait of the blacksmith singer Tío Juane

various forms developed and was mainly performed in gypsy communities, though gypsy singers and dancers were often invited to perform outside them. The early flamenco songs, broadly speaking, appear to have been the *toná*, the *caña*, and the *polo*. The first mentioned may have been the earliest; it was certainly sung by the gypsies in their own style, and it was cited in 1847 by Estébanez Calderón as being performed by the gypsies of Triana. The *toná* also included, under a rather general heading, a number of flamenco songs which would play a key part in the future development of the art: the *martinete*, the *carcelera*, and the *debla*. The *martinete* – the word derives from *martillo* ('hammer') – originated in the blacksmiths' forges, for example in Triana, and had as its subject matter suffering and persecution. In this respect it was related to the *carcelera* – from *cárcel* ('prison') – which was specifically a song of imprisonment. The *debla* – a Sanskrit word meaning 'bright sky' – was probably of religious origin, though little is known of its precise source. Characterized by complex ornamentation, it makes great physical and vocal demands on the singer. As for the *caña* and the *polo,* both may have been transformed into flamenco rather than created by the gypsies.

A crucially important type of song, not specifically mentioned in early references to the *toná* but probably closely related to it, is the *siguiriya*, which came to figure so prominently both in the subsequent evolution of flamenco and in the repertoire of the great flamenco singers. Deriving from the *seguidilla*, a traditional folksong with stanzas of four lines, the *siguiriya* belongs, as far as we know, to the end of the eighteenth and the beginning of the nineteenth century. It was almost always sung by a man and at that time was unaccompanied. Generally regarded as the most emotional type of flamenco song, it is the cry of someone afflicted by destiny – love, betrayal, misfortune or imminent death – a lone voice railing against the stars, as in the following example:

Cuando yo me muera,	*When I come to die,*
te pío un encargo,	*I ask of you one favour,*
que con las trenzas de	*that with the braids of*
[tu pelo negro	*[your black hair*
me marren las manos.	*They tie my hands.*

Along with the *siguiriya*, the *soleá*, which is known to have been sung around 1840 by a celebrated female singer, La Andonda, is usually regarded as forming the true spine of flamenco. The word *soleá* comes from the Spanish word *soledad* ('solitude'); the song itself consists of stanzas of three or, more often, four lines, and its mood can vary from tragic to frivolous, though it is never as dark as that of a *siguiriya*. The following suggests, for example, the irresistible attraction of love despite its attendant ills:

Er querre es cuesta arriba	*To love is all uphill*
y el orvidar, cuesta abajo;	*And to forget is all downhill;*
quiero subir cuesta arriba	*I want to go uphill*
aunque me cueste trabajo.	*Although it cost me dearly.*

Seville, as seen from Triana

The various kinds of flamenco song mentioned above are considered to be the oldest, purest and most serious. They come under the general heading of *cante grande* or *cante jondo* ('deep song'), and are the forms most closely associated with the gypsies. They are also the most difficult and demanding of the singer's physical, vocal and emotional resources.

Gypsy singers in the past were characterized by a rough sound known as a voice *afillá*, particularly suited to expressing the anguish of the songs belonging to the category *cante grande*. The other two broad categories of flamenco song are *cante intermedio* and *cante chico*, neither of them as intense as *cante grande* or requiring a voice *afillá*. *Cante chico*, as the phrase suggests, is the small song, the lightest and brightest of the three categories, while *cante intermedio* falls in between.

During the first half of the nineteenth century, the great centres of flamenco song were Triana (Seville), Cádiz, Jerez, El Puerto de Santa María, Puerto Real, La Isla de San Fernando and Sanlúcar – all towns and cities in south-western Andalusia. Córdoba, Granada and Málaga were less important. Of the main centres, Triana was considered to be the crucible, where quite ordinary and uninteresting musical material was transformed into the pure gold of flamenco. It invariably attracted the most important performers of the time. Cádiz, together with the neighbouring Puerto de Santa María and Puerto Real, had grown in size and population as a result of trade with South America and – more importantly, as far as flamenco was concerned – contained the *barrio* ('district') of Santa María, a gypsy community that produced many famous flamenco singers, especially specialists in the *siguiriya*. They seem to have led a more nomadic existence than those from Triana, travelling to and frequently taking up residence in other towns in southern Andalusia. The third important centre, Jerez, was then as famous for its wine as it is now, and, like Cádiz, housed a gypsy community, the *barrio* of Santiago, from which a host of great flamenco singers emerged. It was, though, the close relationship between these places, their proximity to each other, the interdependence of their gypsy population, and the nature of their shared culture and circumstances, which proved to be the key factor in the development of flamenco. Given all these elements, it is not surprising that flamenco song should have evolved here rather than elsewhere in Spain

The first flamenco singer of which there is any recorded evidence was a certain Tío Luis el de la Juliana. He was thought to have been born in Jerez around 1750, to have been of gypsy origin and a water-seller by profession. The fact that he practised a trade suggests that at this time, and for a long time afterwards, flamenco singers were not professionals in the modern sense, though this is not to say that they did not spend much of their time singing or that they did not get paid for doing so.

Indeed, many of them travelled from one place to another, responding to the demand for their services. They entertained labourers on noblemen's estates, sleeping in the open air and receiving bread and wine in exchange. They sang for the noblemen themselves in their great houses. They performed at wayside inns and taverns, entertaining travellers, labourers, prostitutes, and the rich young men who were 'aficionados' of flamenco. And in towns and villages their voices were heard at fairs, weddings, baptisms and all kinds of celebrations.

A portrait of El Planeta and his characteristic signature

Such would have been the life of the most famous *cantaores* of the first half of the nineteenth century: El Fillo, La Andonda, El Planeta, Frasco el Colorao, Juan Pelao, and María Borrico, all of them born, significantly, in Cádiz, Jerez, or Triana. Francisco Ortega Vargas, commonly known as El Fillo (many flamenco performers were given a nickname), was born in Puerto Real around 1820, though most of his life was spent in Triana. Although he is known to have been an expert in many kinds of flamenco song, his rough voice – the word *afillá* is derived from the name El Fillo – meant that he was perfectly suited to the emotional *siguiriya* for which he was renowned. His life, like that of many other flamenco singers of the time, involved much travelling in pursuit of his art and its financial rewards, as well as *copas* ('cups') of alcohol as a source of inspiration. He died in poverty in 1860, a common enough fate among flamenco singers.

El Fillo's lover, La Andonda, a great flamenco singer in her own right, was especially acclaimed for her singing of *soleares*, considered to be very pure in style and the best kind of flamenco song in Triana. La Andonda seems to have been something of a tigress. She was described by a contemporary as proud, unpredictable, passionate, addicted to alcohol, and fond of fighting with

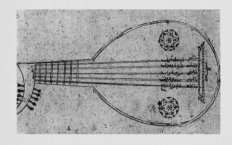

The 'ud' or short-necked lute, from a Persian manuscript; and Moslems and Christians playing the 'guitarra morisca' in a miniature from a Spanish manuscript of the second half of the thirteenth century

OPPOSITE,
The Egyptian element: a dancer from a Coptic tapestry (third to fifth century AD) and another in an Egyptian ivory panel of the eleventh century

a knife – not surprising in the light of the environment in which she lived and the dangers to which she was exposed.

The first description of a flamenco singer was provided by Estébanez Calderón in 1847 when he wrote as follows of El Planeta:

> The newcomer was in truth advanced in years and quite mature: his face was in no way unpleasant: oval shaped with dark, lively, intelligent eyes, a well-shaped nose, a wide mouth and regular white teeth. He had a high forehead, plenty of hair, and a manner which spoke of a certain authority to which no one objected. All these things gave him the outward appearance of some wicked and difficult patriarch...

The ensuing account of El Planeta's clothing – tall narrow-brimmed hat, colourful jacket with embroidered sleeves and silk designs, purple waistcoat and blue trousers – points to the fact that the leading flamenco singers were, indeed, princes of their profession, proud of their fame and their gypsy origins. El Planeta was said to have been skilled at singing all kinds of flamenco song, but particularly noted for his *siguiriyas*, of which the following is sung today:

A la luna le pío,	*I plead with the moon,*
la del alto cielo,	*The one high in the sky,*
cómo le pío que me saque	*How I plead with it to free*
[a mi pare	*[my father*
de onde está metío.	*From where he is imprisoned.*

The reference to the moon here is typical of frequent allusions to the planets in his songs, the origin, it is thought, of his name, El Planeta.

At this stage in the evolution of flamenco, both dance and guitar were of secondary importance. The guitar developed in its modern form from two earlier stringed instruments: the *kithara asiria*, which originated in Egypt and Babylon and was brought to Spain by the Romans; and the *guitarra morisca*, which arrived with the Moors in the eighth century. Up until the middle of the nineteenth century, many types of flamenco song were, however, unaccompanied by the guitar, partly for traditional reasons, partly because guitars were expensive. Its day was still to come.

As for dance, it too remained in the background. Historically, flamenco dance parallels flamenco song in the sense that it has clear connections with India, especially with the Indian classical dance forms of Katak, Kathakali and Bharata Natyam, all of which involve footwork and hand movements which are reminiscent of flamenco.

It seems that Hindu dancers entered Spain by way of Cádiz as early as 500 BC, when they performed for royalty and at particular festivals. Their dances, of an essentially religious nature, later became part of the ceremonies enacted in Roman temples; and later still, during the domination of Spain by the Visigoths from the fifth to the eighth centuries, they were incorporated into the practices of the Christian Church. When the Moors of North Africa invaded the country in 711, beginning their long occupation, these dances began to be performed in a more public and secular way, and were undoubtedly taken up by the Moors themselves, whose own dances were not dissimilar. Considerable emphasis seems to have been placed in the female dance on the movements of the hands, the arms and the upper body, and far less on the feet and the legs, for Islam forbade a woman to reveal or call attention to them. This was something that would become a characteristic feature of the female flamenco dance.

Thus by the time the gypsies came to Spain in numbers in the fifteenth century, there already existed a form of dance with which they, given their

Indian background, could identify. Add to this the co-existence of the gypsies and the persecuted Moors in close-knit communities, and it becomes clear that what later came to be known as flamenco dance developed much as flamenco song did, though the latter was more important.

The words of flamenco songs, like those of the ballads from which they developed, belonged to an oral tradition and did not on the whole appear in print until they were collected and published by particular flamenco enthusiasts in the late nineteenth century. As we have seen, the songs themselves fell into the three broad categories of *cante grande*, *cante intermedio* and *cante chico*, each distinguished from the other by degrees of emotional intensity. But all three shared particular themes – fate, love, the mother figure, death, honour, religion – the essential difference between them being the way those themes were expressed. In *cante grande* the expression is simple, austere, unadorned, the language stripped to a minimum. In *cante intermedio* and *cante chico* it is often more elaborate, more 'poetic', more playful. The following examples will clarify these points, but it is important to understand too that the words of a song on the page give little idea of the way in which it would be performed. Firstly, a flamenco singer shapes a particular song in his own way and much importance is given to improvisation. There is no set music. Secondly, if a guitarist accompanies the singer, he is required to follow the singer wherever the latter's impulse takes him. The vast difference between the words on the page and the style of performance can be gauged from the singing by the great flamenco singer, Manolo Caracol, of the *siguiriya* quoted earlier.

Caracol begins his performance with an introductory ¡Ay!, the lament with which all *siguiriyas* begin but which is not included in the printed text. The ¡Ay! is held for around forty seconds, with two momentary breaks, the final part of it held for around twenty seconds. It is not, however, a single sustained note; rather, the voice wavers and meanders across a series of notes as it expresses the singer's anguish.

Cuando yo me muera,
te pío un encargo,
que con las trenzas de
[tu pelo negro
me marren las manos.

The first half of the first line of the song – 'Cuando yo' – is repeated, the word 'yo' extended in the repeat. The first word of the second half of the line – 'me' – is also extended and then run into 'me muera', which is sustained for about fifteen seconds. The initial 'te' of the second line is drawn out at some length, but the rest of the line – 'pío un encargo'- is abrupt and emphatic, creating a striking contrast.In the third line 'las trenzas' is repeated, and in the second half of the line 'de tu' is extended, as is the final 'o' of 'polo', though the stress in normal speech does not fall on it. In the last line 'me' is extended, but 'marren las manos' is short and dramatic, creating a very emphatic ending.

While the words on the page are relatively flat, the flamenco singer weaves them into a series of intricate arabesques, introducing emphases, repeats and ornamentations which he feels best communicate the emotion of the song. But different singers would, of course, sing the same song in their own way, following their own instinct and improvising accordingly.

Even so, when we hear a virtuoso performance of one of the serious and highly emotional flamenco songs, it is not difficult to understand what the poet and playwright García Lorca meant when he described flamenco song as 'a resonant tear on the river of the voice', observing that in its verses 'Anguish is made flesh'.

Given that the gypsies of Andalusia were a downtrodden and marginalized people, it comes as no surprise to discover that the oldest flamenco songs – those that come under the heading of *cante grande* – express a dark and even tragic mood. The theme of a hostile and inescapable fate is ever present, as in this *soleá*:

An Andalusian gypsy
in a nineteenth-century
photograph

Echada está ya la suerte;	*The die is already cast;*
yo he de seguir mi camino,	*I am to follow my path,*
aunque me lleve a la muerte.	*Although it lead me to death.*

Imprisonment, part of the gypsies' lot, is the typical theme of the *carcelera*:

Veinticinco calabozos	*The prison in Utrera*
tiene la cárcel de Utrera.	*Has twenty-five cells*
Veinticuatro he recorrido	*I have been in twenty-four*
y el más oscuro me queda.	*And the darkest is to come.*

In a *martinete*, sung in the blacksmiths' forges in Triana, the theme is that of a lover tragically deprived of his beloved:

Así, como está la fragua	*Just as the forge becomes*
echa candela de oro,	*A fire of gold,*
se me ponen las entrañas	*So do my insides*
cuando te recuerdo, y lloro.	*When I remember you, and I weep.*

The love theme, too, is central to *cante grande*, usually expressing the lover's despair. In this *siguiriya*, a lover curses the fateful moment in which he and his beloved set eyes on each other:

Reniego de mi sino,	*I curse my fate,*
reniego de ti,	*I curse you,*
como reniego de la horita	*As I curse the hour*
en que te conosí.	*In which I knew you.*

49

In another he expresses his torment as he realizes he has been abandoned:

No quiero que se entere   I don't want her to know,
quien sólo era mía,   She who was mine alone,
que en mis profundos   That in my deep sighs
[suspiros por ella   [for her
se me va la vía.   My life is slipping away.

The frequent appearance of the mother in flamenco song is probably explained by the close-knit character of gypsy communities and of the family within those communities. The following *siguiriya*, for example, suggests that a son's love for his mother is so great that his own troubles are as nothing compared with hers:

Penas tiene mi mare,   My mother has her troubles,
penas tengo yo,   I have mine,
y las que siento son las   And the ones I feel are
[de mi mare,   [my mother's,
que las mas no.   Not my own.

Given the close relationship of mother and son – seemingly almost incestuous at times – her death produces extreme anguish, as in this *siguiriya*:

Se murió la mare mía;   My mother is dead;
ya no hay en er   There are no mothers
[mundo mares,   [in the world
¡mare, la que yo tenía!   Like the mother I used to have!

And yet another expresses his sense of loneliness after her death:

Por una ventana   Through a window
que al campo salía,   Which was facing the fields,
yo daba voces a la mare   I was calling to the mother
[de mi alma   [of my soul
y no me respondía.   And she didn't answer me.

The most important mother of all in flamenco is, though, the Virgin Mary, and many of the *saetas* which accompany the Holy Week processions describe her anguish at the sight of Christ's suffering and imminent death:

A modern flamenco singer

The head of a figure of the 'Christ of Great Power', the work of Juan de Mesa (1620), which is carried in procession on Holy Thursday from Seville Cathedral.

Míralo por onde viene	*Look at him as he comes*
agobiao por el doló,	*Bent double with the pain,*
chorreando por las sienes	*Dripping from his temples*
gotas de sangre y suor.	*Drops of blood and sweat.*
Y su mare de penita	*And his mother in anguish,*
destrosao er corazón.	*Her heart broken.*

Cante grande has something of the dark, austere spirit of Greek tragedy, in particular those songs that rail against the blind and impassive forces which reduce man to a state of helplessness. Their language is equally spare and concise.

The songs of *cante intermedio* have a greater variety of emotion and therefore vary from tragic to frivolous. The following *fandango,* for example, could not be darker in its evocation of despair:

Era jondillo y sin soga	*It was deep and without a rope*
Er poso donde caí,	*The well into which I fell,*
Y por más voces que daba	*And however much I called out*
Nadie me sacó d'allí.	*No one pulled me out of there.*

In a *malagueña* the mood is also dark as an individual curses his fate, but the more literary expression – the simile of the tree – is typical of the distinction between *cante intermedio* and *cante grande*:

Yo soy como el árbol solo	*I am like the solitary tree*
que está en medio del camino,	*Which is half way along the road,*
no tengo calor de naide;	*I have no warmth from anyone;*
¡maldito sea mi sino,	*A curse on my fate,*
que a sufrir no hay quien	*For in suffering there is no one*
[me iguale!	*[who equals me!*

The same kind of literary expression can be found in the following *tiento,* but here the mood is clearly much lighter:

La barca de mis amores	*The ship of my affections*
no teme a los temporales,	*Is not afraid of storms,*
que lleva de marineros	*For it has as its sailors*
los ojitos de mi mare.	*The eyes of my mother.*

And equally light, if somewhat nostalgic, are the songs in praise of towns and cities. Such is this *media granaina* in praise of the city from which the song itself derives its name:

Quiero vivir en Graná	*I want to live in Granada*
porque me gusta el oír	*Because I like to hear*
la campana de La Vela	*The bell of La Vela*
cuando me voy a dormir.	*When I go to sleep.*

Of the three broad categories of flamenco song, *cante chico* contains by far the greatest number of types – around thirty in all. In general, the songs of *cante chico* are bright and cheerful, though this does not mean that the mood cannot sometimes be sombre as the following *fandanguillo* illustrates:

Hasta después de la muerte	*Even after death*
te tengo que estar queriendo,	*I am bound to go on loving you,*
que muerto también se quiere.	*For a man loves too when dead.*
Yo te quiero con el alma,	*I love you with my soul,*
Y el alma nunca se muere.	*And the soul never dies.*

On the other hand, the tone of this *bambera*, in praise of female beauty, could not be brighter:

Eres chiquita y bonita,	*You are tiny and pretty,*
eres como te quiero,	*You are just as I want you,*
eres una campanita	*You are a small bell*
en las manos de un platero.	*In the hands of a silversmith.*

Other songs can be teasingly sensual, as in this *tango*:

Péinate tú con mis peines,	*Comb your hair with my comb,*
que mis peines son de azúca;	*For my comb is made of sugar;*
quien con mis peines se peine,	*Whoever combs his hair with my comb,*
hasta los deos se chupa.	*Will suck his fingers.*

And then there are the lullabies, the *nanas*, usually tender and soothing, and for the singing of which the rocking of the cradle provided the rhythm:

Clavelito encarnado,	*Little pink carnation,*
rosa en capullo,	*Rose yet to bud,*
duérmete, vida mía,	*Sleep now, my treasure,*
mientras te arruyo.	*While I rock you.*

A topic which looms large in any discussion of flamenco performance, and which is extremely difficult to write about with accuracy, is that of *duende*. In ordinary usage the word signifies a mischievous, poltergeist-like spirit, but in the case of flamenco artists it has a rather different meaning. As in most things connected with flamenco, Lorca had much to say about the subject in a lecture called 'Play and Theory of the Duende', which he first gave in Buenos Aires in 1933. He quotes the great *cantaor* Manuel Torre as having observed, while listening to Manuel de Falla play *Nights in the Gardens of Spain*, that 'Whatever has black sounds has *duende*'. For Lorca *duende* was a power which climbed up inside the performer 'from the soles of the feet', the spirit of the earth which scorches the artist and produces an inspired performance. It is, in short, a kind of Dionysian force Lorca closely connected with anguish, mystery and death, which took over the performer, and without which his or her out-pouring would have been merely ordinary. As an illustration of this, Lorca describes a performance by the legendary La Niña de los Peines, which at first was without inspiration. But then she 'downed in one gulp a large glass of aniseed, and began to sing... with a scorched throat... Her voice was no longer playing, her voice was a jet of blood notable for its pain and its sincerity...'

Lorca's definition of *duende* has been dismissed by some as a rather romantic and high-flown explanation of what, in the case of many flamenco performers, was a much more down-to-earth source of inspiration – alcohol and drugs. La Niña de los Peines, by Lorca's own admission, imbibed a good quantity of aniseed and performed with *duende* after doing so. As we have seen, the circumstances in which flamenco developed and the settings in which it was performed – inns and taverns – created between performers and audience a highly charged atmosphere in which inhibitions fell away and, assisted by strong drink, a kind of hysteria prevailed. But, whatever the source, it cannot be denied that the great flamenco singers were often magically inspired. It was said of Manuel Torre that during performance the veins on his forehead stood out and he ripped his clothing as if to release a flood of passion. His face and eyes became wild and his singing irresistible. The flamenco singer Juan Talega observed of Torre that 'Good flamenco song (i.e. "deep song") causes pain, not joy. I have never heard anyone who causes me so much pain. Manuel did fantastic things, Manuel Torre did things that can't be explained... You heard him once and you couldn't get him out of your head...' In short, Manuel Torre sang with *duende*, and the effect on his audience was equally extreme. On one occasion his singing of a *siguiriya* is said to have so aroused his listeners that one of them buried his teeth in Torre's cheek, and on another occasion they became so inflamed that they too ripped their shirts and smashed the chairs.

The singer 'Rancapino' in Seville, 1988

OPPOSITE,
The flamenco singer 'Perefil' in his bar in Seville, 1988

55

All this points to the fact that flamenco song is in a real sense antiaesthetic. The voice of the singer, especially during the early evolution of flamenco, was a voice *afillá*, a rough, typically gypsy voice, or, to use another term, a voice that was *rajo* or hoarse and which no doubt constant singing, smoking and the consumption of alcohol made even rougher. The sound produced by a flamenco singer is often more like a wail or even a howl, and is hardly calculated to appeal to the refined musical taste or to the individual who, lacking any musical taste, aspires to it. Indeed, describing the performance of a gypsy singer near Algeciras in 1955, Laurie Lee noted the way in which his voice resembled 'a naked wail', 'an animal cry, thrown out, as it were, over burning rocks, a call half-lost in air but imperative and terrible'. Antiaesthetic, no doubt, but full of raw and genuine passion.

CHAPTER 2
The evolution of flamenco

THE CAFÉ has an Andalusian patio. It is old and has ceramic tiles, as if they were talismans, with wonderful hieroglyphics designed to bring good luck and ward off the evil eye. The pillars of the patio are Mudejar in style, which in Seville has an air of familiarity, affecting people, things, words and deeds. In the centre is a fountain, and in the fountain a small marble devil, with horns and trident, pees unashamedly onto the backs of sleepy goldfish. The ceiling of the patio is usually the sky itself, but when it gets too hot the opening is covered with a coloured canvas sheet, and in cold weather by a multicoloured sheet of glass... In the patio is the *tablao* and the counter. And the tables are, of course, in the galleries. Above the patio is a rail which separates the world and the underworld, the things which are visible and the things which are hidden and about which one must be silent. To go up there one has to pass through a false door, entering from a street. Up there are the rooms which are reserved. When the show begins, you can see the mysterious shape of someone who, in the company of someone else, looks down, anxious not to be seen, in order to hear and see the singing and dancing. Up there is where the *juerga* will continue when the performance in the *café cantante* is over...

A female flamenco guitarist in the 1890s

In the second half of the nineteenth century flamenco flew the nest, leaving behind its traditional home in gypsy communities and moving into what became known as the *cafés cantantes*. As the phrase suggests, the *café cantante* was a café where flamenco was performed. The owners of ordinary cafés were quick to appreciate both the growing popularity of flamenco and the profits to be made from transforming their premises into venues for its performance. The first *café cantante* of which there is any record existed in Seville in the early 1840s, but the 'golden age' of their popularity occurred between 1860 and 1900 when they flourished not only in Andalusia – in Seville, Cádiz, Jerez, Granada and Málaga – but in other parts of Spain as well, particularly Barcelona and Madrid. The typical *café cantante* had a stage which varied in size, according to the establishment, from a single dais to a much larger

Photograph of a typical
café cantante in Seville,
around 1890

OPPOSITE,
Silverio Franconetti

Frontispiece from
a book devoted to
flamenco song

performance area with a background
of typical Andalusian scenes. There
were tables and chairs for the audience. The *cafés* were lit initially by oil
lamps, later by gaslight. The performers consisted usually of one
or more singers, three or four female
dancers, two male dancers, and a
guitarist. The singer or singers were
splendidly dressed, their hair ele-
gantly groomed. They sported a
cravat or tie, a fine watch-chain, a
colourful handkerchief in the top
pocket of the jacket, and a walking-
stick. Other members of the group
were less ostentatious. They wore tra-
ditional Andalusian costume: the women long dresses and shawls, the men
high-cut jackets and trousers. As for the audience, it was no longer limited to
the gypsies but embraced all social classes, such was the growing appeal of flamenco. For other nationalities, Spain had become a source of fascination, the
Spanish gypsy an archetype of beauty and passion, and flamenco dance the
very embodiment of eroticism. Foreign visitors flocked to the *cafés cantantes*,
as did those Spanish aristocrats who in the past had visited gypsy communities and helped to sponsor the *juergas*. They were frequented too by Spaniards
of all kinds and class.

The rise of the *cafés cantantes* had a significant effect on the character of flamenco itself. They led, inevitably, to a considerable increase in the number of
performers, many of whom now became truly professional, and some no
longer of pure gypsy origin. No doubt as a consequence of this, the pure flamenco songs, which were closely associated with the gypsies and had
dominated the earlier evolution of flamenco (the *siguiriya*, the *soleá*, the *martinete)*, were now accompanied by other styles which had their roots in
Andalusian folklore. In the *cafés*, moreover, flamenco song, which had previously reigned supreme, began to be challenged by flamenco dance, clearly of
popular appeal, easier to appreciate than flamenco song, and well suited to the
theatrical settings and the audiences of these establishments. At the same
time, the guitar started to emerge from its earlier anonymity.

A key figure in this process was Silverio Franconetti, regarded by many as
the most significant flamenco singer of his time. Born in Seville in 1831 of non-
gypsy parents – his father was a prosperous Italian – his ancestry was very

different from that of the singers of the past and in that sense was fairly typical of the new kind of flamenco singer. To be sure, Silverio learned his art from genuine gypsy singers, including El Fillo, and his particular preference was in fact for the old and pure kinds of flamenco at which he excelled. Nevertheless, Silverio was also responsible for certain crucial changes that would take flamenco in a different direction and undermine the status and popularity of *cante grande*.

In the early 1860s Silverio opened in Seville his own *café cantante*, the 'Café Silverio', situated in the Calle del Rosario. It was to become the most famous *café* of its kind, and the description which begins this chapter is a visitor's impression of it. Silverio quickly realized, however, that if flamenco song was to become more accessible to the new and more broadly based audience which attended his establishment, important changes would have to be introduced. He therefore set out to soften the harsh, austere and – in the opinion of many – ugly tone of *cante grande* as it had been sung by his gypsy predecessors. In its place he introduced a softer quality and a greater element of musicality, including the kind of vocal embellishments found in opera, notably light opera, obviously more pleasing to the uninitiated ear. Secondly, he enlarged the existing repertoire of flamenco song by incorporating into it typical Andalusian folksongs. It was a process which can be described as the 'Andalusianization' of the pure flamenco tradition, and one which was seen by the great late-nineteenth-century collector of flamenco songs, Antonio Machado y Alvarez, as destroying flamenco's authenticity. On the other hand, the period dominated by Silverio and a number of other great singers has not been described as the Golden Age of Flamenco without reason, and the point has been made that if, in the process of 'Andalusianization', flamenco lost its former purity, Andalusian folksongs benefited greatly by becoming 'gypsified' and adapted to flamenco style. The influence of Silverio and the *cafés cantantes* was positive in another way: not only did the singers who performed there become much more professional; they also achieved the fame and status which made them stars of the flamenco circuit.

Another key figure in this process was the blind flamenco singer Antonio Ortega Escalona, better known as Juan Breva. Born in Vélez-Málaga in 1844 to a peasant

Juan Breva, the blind singer known as the 'King of the *malagueñas*'

family, he was, like Silverio, a non-gypsy and also an agent for the infiltration of Andalusian folksong into the ancient and pure territory of *cante grande*. In particular, he helped to popularize the folksong known as the *malagueña*, which, as its name indicates, had its origin not in the homeland of *cante grande* – Seville, Cádiz, Jerez – but in Málaga. The subject matter of this kind of song was generally serious and its tone, as sung by the great flamenco singers, quite dramatic:

En ti puse mi querer	*In you I placed all my love*
creyendo que ya eras buena	*Believing that you were good*
pero yo me equivoqué;	*But I made a great mistake;*
tú sigues siendo quien eras	*You are still the same as you were*
y Dios te lo pague, mujer.	*And may God pay you for it, woman.*

Nevertheless, the *malagueña* was not true *cante grande*, and Juan Breva's success in making it so popular struck another blow at the older forms of flamenco song. In addition, many of the old-style singers quickly realized that fame and fortune could be achieved by singing *malagueñas*, so they abandoned the old in favour of the new. As for Juan Breva, he became known as the 'King of the *malagueñas*' and achieved enormous fame, starring in 1884 at three venues in Madrid, including the Teatro Príncipe Alfonso, and singing in the presence of the King and Queen. Like many flamenco performers, however, he wasted his money, and it is said that at the end of life he was obliged to sing to be able to pay for his funeral.

Although the incursion of Andalusian folksong into the territory of flamenco weakened the older form's supremacy, it did not destroy it; rather, there developed in the evolution of flamenco song between 1850 and 1930 a gypsy, non-gypsy duality. Apart from Silverio and Juan Breva, the non-gypsy singers (they were known as *payos*) included Fosforito, Antonio Chacón, Manuel Vallejo, José Cepero, Cayetano Muriel, Aurelio Sellé, and La Trini. The gypsy hierarchy comprised El Fillo, Tomás el Nitri, Manuel Molina, Manuel Cagancho, Loco Mateo, Curro Durse, Enrique el Mellizo, Manuel Torre, Tomás Pavón and Pastora Pavón. The singers of gypsy origin generally clung to their own traditions and therefore specialized in *cante grande* – *siguiriyas, soleares, martinetes, carceleras* – while non-gypsy singers revealed a preference for songs that originally belonged to the Andalusian folk tradition – *malagueñas, verdiales, granadinas, fandangos* – and which, even though adapted to the flamenco style, were performed in a way that lacked the harshness of the genuine gypsy voice *afillá*. In this respect Tomás el Nitri was as much a true representative of the gypsy tradition as was Silverio of the *payo*.

Born in 1850, probably in Puerto de Santa Maria and of genuine gypsy stock, Tomás el Nitri's rivalry with Silverio was such that, in spite of the latter's requests, Tomás would never sing in his presence. Not surprisingly, he was famous for his singing of the older forms, notably the *siguiriya*, to which his frequent black moods were suited. His gypsy origins are also clearly suggested by the fact that, like the old gypsy singers, he was always on the move, travelling from place to place for his performances. His death occurred in an appropriately dramatic and premature fashion in 1890 when, already

Tomás el Nitri

weakened by tuberculosis, he choked on his own blood during the performance of a *siguiriya*.

The *cafés cantantes* also witnessed the increasing popularity of flamenco dance and, over a period of time, its growing complexity in terms of movement, footwork and repertoire. Before considering particular dancers and the evolution of the dance itself, it is, however, important to note that, like flamenco song, flamenco dance falls into three broad categories: *baile grande*, *baile intermedio*, and *baile chico*. The first of these contains the slower and most serious dances, corresponding to the serious songs of *cante grande*. The second, *baile intermedio*, has some of those elements but is lighter in general, and the third, *baile chico*, is characterized by altogether more joyful and lively dances which require rapid footwork and arm movements. All three categories may be performed by either men or women, but mixed dancing is also common.

The essential movements of the dance have been described in some detail by Donn Pohren. In *baile grande* and *baile intermedio* the male dancer, the *bailaor*, holds his body straight, bending backwards a little, his arms curved. The emphasis in the dance is placed on his legs, his footwork is strong, and the

total effect is one which suggests the dignity, the manliness and the passion of both the dancer and the dance itself. The rhythm is frequently marked by finger snapping, known as *pitos*. As for the female dancer, the *bailaora*, the movement of the upper body, arms and hands are all key elements in both *baile grande* and *baile intermedio*. The arms are raised to form an elegant curve, and the hands are frequently used to make beautiful circular movements. The body is arched backwards from the waist, the hips are moved gracefully but without exaggeration, and the expression is serious, in accordance with the gravity of the dance. In these serious dances the *bailaora* moves but little off a given spot, *zapateado* – the stamping of the feet – is relatively infrequent, finger snapping sometimes plays an important part, but castanets are never used because they would distract from the graceful movement of hands and arms. *Baile chico*, on the other hand, is full of exuberance. There is much more humour, footwork is faster and lighter, finger snapping and clapping – *palmas* – emphasize the rhythm, and the overall mood is of unrestrained joy.

Mixed dancing, which involves two or three dancers and sometimes more, may be serious or light. It communicates not the feelings of a single individual but the emotional reactions of two or three people towards each other: love, jealousy, hate. A dialogue between two lovers, be it teasing or angry, can be suggested purely by *zapateado* or by the sound of castanets. Mixed dancing is particularly effective in relation to telling a story, as in the case of many modern flamenco shows.

For the most part, though, flamenco dance – especially *baile grande* and *baile intermedio* – is an essentially solo activity which depends for its successful expression upon the inner, emotional resources of the performer. Classical ballet is in many ways the opposite, for it requires precise technique and athleticism rather than something which comes from within. Because of this, it demands large performance spaces, and its practitioners are usually young. Flamenco, on the other hand, can be danced on a very small stage or even on a smallish table, and because it calls for experience and maturity rather than athleticism, its exponents continue to dance at an age which no ballet dancer can possibly contemplate. Like flamenco song, the dance will also benefit greatly if the performer is inspired by *duende*, that Dionysian power which drives the

Drawing of a dancing gypsy woman by Ricardo Canals

OPPOSITE,
A modern flamenco dancer in a *tablao* in Seville; and an 1882 painting by John Singer Sargent called 'El Jaleo'

'Fandango', a coloured woodcut by Ferdinand von Rosnicek, 1906

artist to produce an exceptional performance. It need not follow, though, that the latter is a thing of beauty, for what matters most is the dance's power to move, to excite, and this, like flamenco song, may involve a certain roughness.

The dancers who performed in the *cafés cantantes* between 1840 and 1900 provide clear evidence both of the difference between the male and the female dance and of its gradual evolution in terms of its repertoire and complexity. Most of the early dancers were of gypsy origin and their range and technique were predictably limited in comparison to those of their successors. Such was Miracielos, born in Cádiz around 1800, who became famous in the *cafés* between 1840 and 1850. He was especially noted for his strong footwork in the *zapateado*, in which the feet drum on the floor and the body is held rigid, and in certain forms of *alegrías*. The earliest female dancers of whom there is firm evidence were Rosario la Honrá, born around 1845, and Josefita la Pitraca, born in Cádiz some ten years later. They used almost no footwork, concentrating instead on the movement of the hands, arms and the upper body – a throwback to the attitude of the Moors towards the display of female legs and feet.

The rather primitive and restricted nature of flamenco dance persisted until around 1900 when several male dancers appeared on the scene. Antonio el de Bilbao, a non-gypsy, was born around 1880 in Seville. Trained as a classical dancer, he became famous in the *cafés cantantes* for his fast and complex footwork, and on one occasion in Seville is said to have performed a twenty-minute *zapateado* which left the audience astonished. Strong and expressive footwork was also associated with Francisco Mendoza Ríos, better known as Faico; Juan Sánchez Valencia el Estampío; and Antonio López Ramírez, generally known as Ramirito – all three born in the early 1880s. Faico and Ramirito also extended the existing repertoire by dancing the *farruca*, an essentially male dance which asserted dignity and masculinity and was characterized by a strong element of *zapateado*. El Estampío too excelled in this aspect of the dance, but he differed from his contemporaries in his expressive hand and arm movements, a skill acquired no doubt from his female dance teacher. Bit by bit, then, technique became bolder and more varied and new dances were introduced.

The same was largely true of the female dancers of this time, two of whom were particularly famous. Juana Vargas la Macarrona, of gypsy origin, was born in Jerez around 1860 and is often said to have been the greatest female flamenco dancer of her time. At the age of sixteen she was already appearing at the Café Silverio in Seville in the company of the famous singers of the day, including Silverio himself. She also danced at the Café Burrero in the same city and at the Café Romero in Madrid, before undertaking engagements in other European countries. Proof of the fact that flamenco dancers do not need to be young, she continued to dance to the age of eighty. Her contemporary, Rosario Monje la Mejorana, born in Cádiz around 1862, also became famous at the Café Silverio and is thought to have added to the repertoire by introducing the slow and beautiful *baile por soleá*. But despite more sophisticated

Antonio de Bilbao in performance, 1930s
La Macarrona and the featured guitarist
Niño Ricardo in the 1930s

technique and an element of innovation, both these dancers employed little footwork, concentrating instead on the movement of hands, arms and upper body and thereby retaining those traditional aspects of the female dance.

As was the case with dance, the first truly professional and accomplished guitarists also began to appear in conjunction with the development of the *cafés cantantes*. Prior to this, many types of flamenco song were performed without guitar accompaniment, and even when guitarists were involved, they were for the most part accompanists. In the *cafés cantantes* they quickly increased in number and became more polished in technique, for they were now required to perform much more often and to accompany many different kinds of flamenco song and dance, from *cante* and *baile grande* to *cante* and *baile chico*. As professionals they also had more time to improve their technique, and the more of them there were, the sharper the sense of competition among them. It was not long, therefore, before particular individuals became virtuosi of the guitar and stars of the *cafés cantantes* in which they regularly performed – as much soloists in their own right as the flamenco singers and dancers, well paid and just as famous.

As in the case of flamenco song and flamenco dance, flamenco guitar also falls into three categories: *toque grande*, *toque intermedio* and *toque chico*, the character of the music within these categories corresponding largely to their equivalents in the song and the dance. It is also important to know the meaning of some of the terms used in relation to the guitar, all of them explained in detail by Donn Pohren but described more simply here. The word *falseta* refers to a melody or a melodic variation which, in the case of a guitarist accompanying a singer, may be introduced to give the singer time to recover if he needs to pause, or if his performance is not of the best. *Compás* means simply 'rhythm' or 'beat' and is particularly important in any flamenco guitarist's performance, not least in the accompaniment to flamenco song when the singer's freedom to improvise means that the guitarist is obliged to follow wherever taken. *Rasgueado* – *rasguear* is to 'strum' – describes the running of the fingers over the strings in a continuous motion. *Pulgar* ('thumb') refers to the technique of using the thumb of the same hand to strike individual strings in sequence, and *picado*, *arpegio* and *trémolo* allude to other finger movements. The first of these involves the index and middle fingers alternately striking a string. An *arpegio* consists of the thumb striking a bass string, while two or even three fingers alternately strike treble strings. And a *trémolo* refers to the thumb striking a bass string, while two, three, or even four fingers alternately strike a treble string. Finally, the term *ligado* is used of a technique involving the hand other than that used for the procedures described above. It describes the action of moving a finger down and off a string in order to produce a slurring effect. These techniques produce the dramatic chording and intricate arabesques of a skilled guitarists's performance, and illustrate how, during the period of the *cafés cantantes*, the guitarists expanded the potentialities of their instrument.

When they had acted mainly as accompanists, they had concentrated on *rasgueado*, *pulgar* and *picado* in the case of the right hand, and on *ligados* in the case of the left. With the advent of the *cafés*, the more difficult techniques of *arpegios* and *trémolos* were added, the decorative capacity of the guitar increased, and its emotional range became greater. El Maestro Patiño, born around 1829, and Antonio Pérez, some six years younger, both played in Seville in the early days of the *cafés* solely as accompanists to singers and dancers. The increasing importance of the guitar can, however, be seen in the fact that one of El Maestro Patiño's pupils, Paco el Barbero, quickly turned from accompaniment to solo performance and enjoyed such success that he was able to retire and open his own flamenco tavern. But the first true virtuoso of the guitar was Francisco Díaz, who was born in 1855 in Lucena in the province of Córdoba and who was therefore known as Paco Lucena. The son of a farm hand, he became proficient in both flamenco and classical techniques and, having commenced his career as an accompanist in the *cafés cantantes* in Málaga, moved to the prestigious Café Silverio in Seville, where he muchpreferred to play solo. His knowledge of the classical guitar meant that he was able to introduce certain classical techniques into his performance of flamenco, thereby extending its range of expression. He is said to have

Spanish dancers and a guitarist photographed in 1890 in Seville

amazed audiences with his skill, which included the trick of playing with his left hand covered with a glove.

Two other guitarists who played in the *cafés* in the early part of their career and also made significant contributions to the development of the instrument in solo performance were Javier Molina and Ramón Montoya. Born in Jerez in 1868, Molina became one of the stars of both the Café Silverio and the Café Burrero over a period of twenty years, performing as accompanist and soloist. Montoya, born in Madrid around 1880, has been described as the first guitar virtuoso for virtuosity's sake. Like Paco Lucena, he had a sound knowledge of the classical guitar but made a much greater contribution than his predecessor in incorporating classical elements into flamenco. Indeed, Ramón Montoya, more than anyone, took the flamenco guitar into its modern period and style.

The next stage in the evolution of flamenco occurred in the early part of the twentieth century when the tradition of the *cafés cantantes* began to decline. Many of them were by this time associated with the less desirable elements of society and were closed down for that reason. Consequently, flamenco moved into other

Enrique el Mellizo

areas and venues, and in the process underwent fundamental changes which, between 1910 and 1950, further weakened its traditional character and made it much more commercial. If during the period of the *cafés cantantes* flamenco song was 'Andalusianized' by the incorporation of the folksong tradition, it was now popularized and in many ways vulgarized by its movement into the world of the theatre.

One of the most significant figures in this respect was Antonio Chacón, who was born in Jerez in 1869. Although not a gypsy, his love of flamenco song was acquired from the gypsy *cantaores* of his home town, and the older and purer kinds of song were his true preference. His favourite singers, including Enrique el Mellizo from whom he learned much, were all experts in those forms. But Chacón suffered from the great disadvantage that he did not possess the typically harsh gypsy voice and could not therefore exploit the full potential of *cante grande*. For that reason he chose to specialize in *cante intermedio* in particular and, as Juan Breva had done before him, made the *malagueña* the cornerstone of his art, for it suited his sweet and melodious voice. He refined flamenco song in other ways, replacing its rather rough and often idiomatic gypsy language with grammatically correct Spanish. As a result of such innovations, the general public began to regard *cante grande* as crude, harsh and primitive, and so turned their back on it.

Although Chacón sang initially in the *cafés cantantes*, the venues in which he performed at the height of his career were very different indeed. Apart from starring in theatre shows of an essentially popular nature, he often sang for the aristocracy at refined and elegant establishments where flamenco was now regularly presented. He performed at country houses and palaces; entertained the Spanish dictator General Miguel Primo de Rivera; sang on numerous occasions in the 1920s at the Royal Palace; and in 1924 arranged flamenco entertainment for the visiting King and Queen of Italy. In short, Chacón made flamenco socially respectable and in so doing became the first gentleman *cantaor*; even the King of Spain referred to him as Don Antonio Chacón, a prefix which confirmed his standing as an aristocrat among aristocrats. He was indeed the 'King of flamenco', and by far the best-paid singer of the time. But there can be no doubt that, even if his own performance standards were very high, Chacón's success in popularizing flamenco song seriously weakened it. In the theatre, for example, it came to be combined with dance and even with ballet, or integrated into the form of Spanish light opera known as *zarzuela*. In other words, it became increasingly shallow and frivolous.

Antonio Chacón, a leading singer of the golden age of flamenco, and his main rival, Manuel Torre

Nevertheless, there were still many great singers of *cante grande*, even if they tended now to sing in the original locations of flamenco – taverns, fiestas, and celebrations of different kinds. One of the very greatest was Manuel Soto Loreto, born in Jerez in 1878 and more commonly known as Manuel Torre, a nickname inherited from his equally tall father. His passionate and unpredictable nature meant that he was ideally suited to the performance of *cante grande*. As a young man, for example, he was so moved by the singing of Enrique el Mellizo that he broke down in tears and threatened to leap from an open window. On another occasion, listening to the same singer, he apparently bit through the glass from which he was drinking. But if he was himself deeply moved by the older forms of flamenco song, he was also capable of inspiring similar emotions in his audience, reducing it to a state of hysteria. The reason for this lay largely in his emotional temperament and his total command of his art, but it also had much to do with the nature of his voice. He was the first flamenco singer to sing with a *voz natural*, a 'natural voice', in which the sound came predominantly from the chest, and the harshness which characterized the *voz afillá*, the typical gypsy voice, was less evident. Indeed, Manuel Torre's style of singing had the effect of largely replacing that tradition.

Inevitably, though thirteen years younger, he proved to be Antonio Chacón's greatest rival, and comparisons between them

have often been made. A contemporary of both, Fernando el de Triana, considered that Chacón had a more pleasing voice but that Torre's appeal to the emotions was more direct; and Juan Talega, who knew both men, preferred Torre's rawer and more primitive style. The difference between them reveals, in effect, the great divide that was becoming more and more evident in flamenco in general: on the one hand, the softer and more refined flamenco song which, embodied in Chacón, appealed to a wider audience; on the other, the older, rougher forms which, represented by Manuel Torre, survived in their more traditional and restricted locations. And, as far as the latter were concerned, there were other famous singers who played their part: Pepe de la Matrona, Tomás Pavón, Pastora Pavón la Niña de los Peines, Manolo Caracol, and Antonio Mairena, to name only a few.

It is appropriate in this context to mention the Festival of 'Deep Song', which took place in Granada in 1922 and at which, even though they did not participate, many of the most famous flamenco performers of the time were present, including Manuel Torre, Antonio Chacón, Pastora Pavón, la Niña de los Peines, and Juana Vargas la Macarrona. The aim of the festival competition was to save the older and purer forms of flamenco song from the rapid decline occasioned by the *cafés cantantes* and, more recently, the theatres. To this end, the organizers invited performers from the whole of Andalusia to enter, but insisted that they should not be professionals and that they should perform only songs which belonged to *cante grande*. At the end of two days of open-air performance, attended by a large and colourfully dressed audience in the Alhambra's Plaza de los Aljibes, two prize-winners were named. The first was Diego Bermúdez Cala, nicknamed El Tenazas ('Pincers'), an old man of 68 who had walked the eighty miles from his home in Puente Genil in order to take part. Reputed to have given up singing some thirty years earlier on account of a stab-wound in one lung, he had modelled his style on that of Silverio Franconetti, and on the first day of the competition sang two impressive *siguiriyas*. On the second day he was less effective, having consumed too much alcohol on the previous night. The other prize-winner could not have been more different: he was the twelve-year-old Manolito Ortega who, as Manolo Caracol, would become one of the truly great flamenco singers. His success in the competition proved to be the beginning of a long and highly successful career in which he sang all over Spain, often in the presence of very distinguished people.

Though well intentioned, the Granada festival largely failed to achieve its aims. The truly professional flamenco singers were, after all, on the sidelines – acting as judges or in the audience – and the amateurs who took part were not, with some exceptions, very good. Although El Tenazas subsequently per-

Ticket for the 'Deep Song' Festival in Granada in June 1922

Emilia Llanos, a friend of Lorca, dressed for the 'Deep Song' competition

formed in various flamenco shows which were intended to continue the spirit and achievement of the competition, the experience was short-lived and he soon returned to his home town where he died in poverty in 1933. It was left to the professionals to fight for the survival of true flamenco song in the face of a rising tide of mediocrity.

Part of this mediocrity was José Tejada Martín, a non-gypsy from Marchena in the province of Seville, better known as Pepe Marchena. He proved at an

The dancer Aurora la Cujiní; a popular print from Seville

A performance of Opera Flamenca in 1928, featuring among others Antonio Chacón, La Niña de los Peines, Manuel Vallejo and the guitarists Ramón Montoya and Luis Yance

early age to be an excellent singer of the kind of flamenco favoured by Chacón, but soon began to mix different kinds of flamenco song, to add elements which had nothing to do with true flamenco, and even to sing flamenco to an orchestral accompaniment. Specializing in the less serious forms, he adapted them to his own ends, introduced all manner of vocal embellishments, and, worst of all, sang popular songs in the flamenco style. By these means he became a household name and made a fortune.

Another stage in the process of decline concerned the growing popularity of the so-called *ópera flamenca*. It was, as the name suggests, an entertainment which owed something to opera, and because its main purpose was commercial it was generally presented in large venues, including bullrings, to as large an audience as possible. The orchestra became an important part of the performance, and the guitar, so significant previously, became merely one instrument among many. Flamenco song itself was subordinated to a dramatic action or plot, and the older forms, considered too serious and therefore unsuited to popular entertainment, were rejected in favour of the lighter, which were thought to be more pleasing. In addition, the Andalusian *cuplé* or popular song was adapted to the flamenco style. Singers organized themselves into companies and took their 'shows' from town to town and city to city. Voices were clear, well trained and frequently falsetto, very different indeed from the traditional flamenco voice. Even so, because *ópera flamenca* now ruled the roost and progressively pushed old-style flamenco into the background, many of the traditional singers were tempted to abandon their prejudices and jump on the bandwagon.

A good example of the move towards *ópera flamenca* is a company formed in 1926 that included the flamenco guitarists Javier Molina, Ramón Montoya, Luis Yance and Niño Ricardo; the flamenco dancer Juana la Macarrona; and the flamenco singers El Cojo de Málaga, Manuel Centeno, and Pastora Pavón La Niña de los Peines, all of them experts in the older flamenco forms. An account of the tour undertaken by this group reveals that it visited many of the large towns and cities in the south and south-east of Spain: Alicante, Ciudad Real, Córdoba, Elche, Granada, Málaga and Murcia.

The venues in which it performed – theatres and bullrings – did violence to the close contact between performers and audience that is so necessary. In this respect the participation of La Niña de los Peines in the company is particularly interesting because it throws light on the dilemma confronting performers who were previously committed to traditional flamenco.

Here was someone unsurpassed in that tradition, a woman who, unusually, sang *siguiriyas* in the most moving and convincing manner, had a complete command of every kind of flamenco song, yet sometimes took part in *ópera flamenca*.

The most charitable explanation for the involvement of such great artists in these spectacles is that they were tempted to try their hand at something new, though it seems quite likely that they did so largely for financial gain. Much more typical of the new style of flamenco was Miguel Sampedro Montero Angelillo, who became one of *ópera flamenca*'s stars and whose repertoire consisted entirely of *cante chico* forms – *milongas, colombianas, guajiras* and *fandanguillos* – which were better suited to his falsetto voice.

Similarly successful was Juanito Valderrama who, despite his knowledge of and ability in the purer kinds of flamenco song, introduced into his television performances such novelties as the 'flamenco twist' and the 'flamenco cha-cha-cha', as well as popular songs adapted to flamenco rhythms. Needless to say, singers of this kind made many recordings, earning them even more money.

The decline of the *cafés cantantes* and the movement of flamenco in general into theatre spaces also had a fundamental effect on flamenco dance. In the first place, the number and range of dances increased dramatically, largely because songs which in the past had been regarded as sacrosanct – such as the *siguiriya* – were now adapted to the dance. A dance to the rhythm of the *siguiriya* therefore became known as a *baile por siguiriyas*, that to the rhythm of a *martinete* as a *baile por martinetes*. In addition, castanets came into use, even though purists considered them alien to true flamenco because they inhibited the movements of the hands and arms, a key element in the female dance. And in certain respects the female dance itself changed. Some female dancers

introduced intricate and elaborate footwork, previously the prerogative of the male dance, and wore male costume, abandoning the traditional *bata de cola* dress with its flounced train. To a large extent commercial flamenco had the effect of stifling improvisation, for performers were now required to dance night after night and to develop, therefore, that kind of precision which had never previously been part of the dance. And finally, the creation of large theatrical companies undermined flamenco dance itself in favour of what came to be known as the *ballet español*, a mixture of classical, regional and flamenco dances performed by classical dancers who were also able to dance a refined form of flamenco. The direct result of this was that the *ballet español*, or *ballet flamenco* as it was also known, was soon considered by many to be genuine flamenco. It became both extremely popular and profitable while, up until about 1950, flamenco song and dance themselves suffered a marked decline.

Two male dancers who achieved great fame during this period and illustrate these points were Vicente Escudero and Antonio Ruiz Soler (known simply as Antonio). Escudero, a non-gypsy born in 1895 in Valladolid, began dancing in the *cafés cantantes* but, as they began to decline, moved into the world of the theatre, performing in the *fines de fiesta* – acts offered in the intervals and at the end of theatre shows – and in the *ballet flamenco*. He was, in fact, like many others at this time, both a *bailaor* (a flamenco dancer) and a *bailarín* (a ballet dancer). In flamenco dance he expanded the repertoire considerably by adapting flamenco songs to dance technique, as in the case of the *siguiriya*, defending such innovations on the grounds that they were justified if done with reverence and good taste. To his great credit, he avoided cheap tricks even though he refused to be bound by traditional rules.

Antonio, more famous internationally than Escudero, was born in Seville in 1922. Although his work was largely commercial and involved a good deal of classical Spanish dance, he was also an excellent flamenco dancer who, despite the strict discipline of his classical training, had the ability to introduce spontaneity and improvisation into his performance of flamenco. He possessed both excellent footwork and graceful, expressive arm and upper body movement. Like Escudero, he was also an innovator, creating the *baile por mar-*

Carmen Amaya was probably the most widely known and admired female flamenco dancer of modern times. Here she is in Paris in 1959.

OPPOSITE,
The dancer Vicente Escudero at the height of his fame in 1928; portrait by Man Ray

tinetes from the rhythm of the flamenco song that had traditionally been sung in the blacksmiths' forges. And he was one of the first flamenco dancers to engage in mixed dancing, which subsequently became an accepted feature of flamenco. His regular partner was Florencia Pérez Padilla, commonly known as Rosario. As 'Los Chavalillos de España' she and Antonio danced all over the world until 1952, when they formed their own separate companies, with which they continued to enjoy great success.

The female dancers of the time also bear witness to significant changes in the dance. Pastora Imperio, born in Seville in 1890, began dancing in the *fines de fiesta* at the age of eleven and subsequently formed her own flamenco group, which frequently featured such great performers as the guitarist Ramón Montoya and the singer Manuel Torre. Despite her association with the theatres, Pastora Imperio favoured the more traditional female dance, with its emphasis on the arms and upper body, and in this respect was rather different from her contemporaries. Two of these, Antonia Mercé la Argentina and Encarnación López la Argentinita, were closely associated with the *ballet español*. Antonia Mercé, born around 1886, specialized in the new, refined, more classical kind of dance and was an expert in the use of castanets, of which Pastora Imperio would have strongly disapproved. La Argentinita, some fourteen years younger, was initially unfamiliar with flamenco dance but learned to perform particular dances bit by bit. The theatre piece *Las calles de Cádiz* (*The Streets of Cadiz*), which she staged very successfully in 1933, illustrates the way in which traditional flamenco was now being incorporated into theatrical spectacle, though in this particular case it was done with integrity and taste. Set in the gypsy quarter of Cádiz, the barrio Santa María, *Las calles* involved leading flamenco performers, including the great dancer La Macarrona, then in her seventies. Each artist performed his or her role in true flamenco style, with inspiration and spontaneity, and in that respect *Las calles de Cádiz* can be seen as a forerunner of the theatre shows presented

nowadays by the companies of Cristina Hoyos, Antonio Gades, and Paco Peña.

Special mention must be made too of Carmen Amaya, regarded by many as the greatest female dancer of the twentieth century. Born in 1913 in the gypsy area of Somorrostro, on the edge of Barcelona, she began to dance in public at the age of four and by seven was performing in the theatres. When she was ten she was involved with flamenco groups that contained such famous stars as Manuel Torre and La Niña de los Peines. At sixteen she danced at the International Exhibition in Barcelona, and subsequently appeared in many foreign cities, including those in North, Central and South America. More dynamic than any of the female dancers mentioned earlier, Carmen Amaya introduced into the female dance the fast and exciting footwork which had previously been the speciality of male dancers, and she also often wore the man's short jacket, shirt and trousers. On the other hand, as her style devel-

OPPOSITE,
La Argentina (Antonia Mercé), appearing in *ballet español*

Pastora Imperio; illustration on a poem dedicated to her

La Argentina

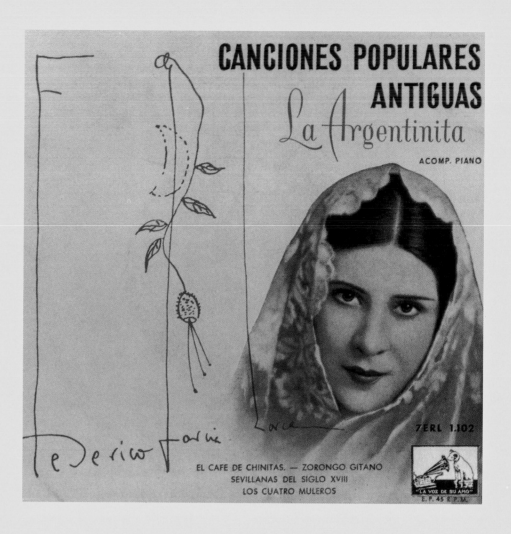

EL CAFE DE CHINITAS. — ZORONGO GITANO
SEVILLANAS DEL SIGLO XVIII
LOS CUATRO MULEROS

La Argentinita
(Encarnación López
Júlvez): a record sleeve

OPPOSITE,
A 1939 poster for
Carmen, performed
in Mexico by Carmen
Amaya, 'prodigy of the
art of flamenco'

oped, she also preserved the traditional elements of the female dance, thereby combining masculine and feminine elements in a unique way, and in that respect preparing the way for the female dancers we see performing today.

Although song, dance and guitar are the three principal elements of flamenco performance, it is important to bear in mind a number of other vital aspects, each of them percussive and important in its own way. Castanets, as we have seen, were never a part of flamenco dance in the early days of its evolution, even though they had existed throughout the Mediterranean from early Christian times. Frowned upon by dancers such as Pastora Imperio for the reasons already mentioned, they were favoured by others and are undoubtedly suited to the lighter, quicker, exuberant dances of *baile chico*, as well as to the regional folk dances which are loosely grouped together under the general heading of flamenco – *sevillanas, fandangos de Huelva, verdiales*. The sound of the castanets greatly enlivens the rhythm of the dance itself.

Another familiar percussive element is hand clapping, known as *palmas*, in which there are two contrasting techniques. The first consists of the three middle fingers of one hand being struck against the open palm of the other to

¡CARMEN

Para
Carmen Amaya
Prodigio del arte
flamenco,,

con la admiración
y afecto de

(Ruano Llopis)
México-VI.
939

produce a sharp, precise sound; the second involves the cupped palms of both hands being brought together to produce an altogether more muffled sound. Rapid clapping, frequently used as an accompaniment to dance, is well suited to the quicker rhythms and is known as *palmas fuertes*. Cupped palms, more appropriate to the slower rhythms, are called *palmas sordas*. Another familiar feature – finger snapping or *pitos* – is employed to mark rhythm. And finally, hands or knuckles are often used to beat out a rhythm on a wooden surface, be it some kind of box or a table top. There is no better example of this than in the tobacco factory scene in Carlos Saura's film, *Carmen*, where the beating of female hands on tables sets in motion a brilliant episode in which all the separate elements of flamenco – *palmas*, *zapateado*, song, dance – combine and interweave to a point where the excitement becomes almost unbearable and the skill of the performers breathtaking.

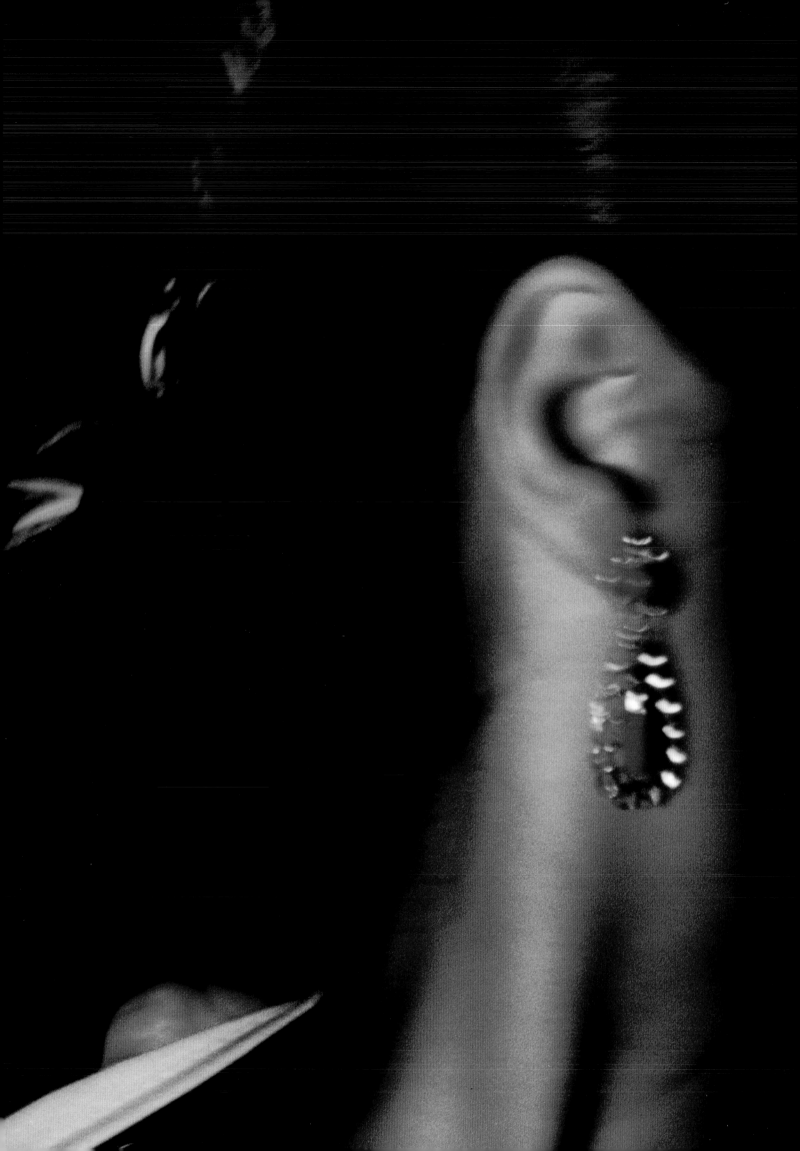

CHAPTER 3
Flamenco renaissance

IF THE MOVEMENT of flamenco into *cafés cantantes* and then theatres seriously weakened its pure and time-honoured character, the triumph of the Nationalists in the Spanish Civil War and the commencement of the thirty-six-year Franco dictatorship in 1939 threatened it with virtual extinction. This was not, however, because the Nationalists were necessarily opposed to a tradition so closely associated with the gypsies – an ethnic minority that could hardly be popular with the right wing – but rather because they saw flamenco as an example of an authentic and colourful Spain which they could exploit both to entertain foreign visitors and to suggest to the world at large that the horrors of the Civil War were things of the past. It was the same kind of camouflage often applied earlier. In the early part of the century the brothers Serafín and Joaquín Alvarez Quintero, two of Spain's most popular and successful dramatists, had created in their work a colourful and charming picture of Andalusia which gave no hint of the enormous social and economic problems that beset its people. In presenting dancing girls in polka-dot costumes on stages in cities, towns and coastal resorts, the Nationalists sought to do much the same, but the result was the reduction of flamenco to a superficial entertainment. Where in such shows was the anguish that lies at the heart of genuine flamenco song, or the beauty and gravity which are such a fundamental feature of much flamenco dance? In the hands of the Nationalists, flamenco became a propaganda tool with which to cheer up Spaniards themselves as well as to provide pretty pictures for tourists who, in any case, would not know better.

Poster of the Seville
Spring Feria in 1947

Given this context, it is astonishing that a flamenco renaissance should have commenced around 1950, but less surprising that this should have been associated, at least in part, with events outside rather than inside Spain. Spanish dance companies that toured abroad often featured outstanding performers – singers as well as dancers and guitarists – who made a considerable impression on foreign audiences and created in them an enormous enthusiasm for flamenco. Paradoxically, the presentation of flamenco in theatres, which had earlier diluted its genuine quality, proved now to be the source of its regeneration. Foreign enthusiasts, eager to discover more about what for them was a new experience, began going to Spain to track it down in its proper

Poster of the Seville
Spring Feria in 1955

setting. As a result, many of the living old-style, non-commercial performers who had virtually retired in despair were suddenly rediscovered. The process was also assisted by impresarios who arranged foreign tours and by leading recording companies who contracted flamenco artists, particularly singers, to record anthologies of flamenco song. Many of these singers were older men and women versed in the flamenco forms most in danger of disappearing. These at last acquired a permanent existence on record, and the pure forms of *cante grande* became familiar to a new and enthusiastic public.

Although the recordings were available in France, the United States and other countries before they appeared in Spain, their arrival on the Spanish market had a decisive impact. Spaniards themselves began to learn something of *flamenco puro*, and singers who had either become disillusioned or who were unacquainted with those older forms began to perform them. It was truly an awakening to the glories of flamenco's past.

At more or less the same time the flamenco night clubs known as *tablaos* began to appear – the word *tablao* meaning stage and by extension the venue in which flamenco was presented. The first of these was La Zambra, which opened in Madrid in 1954 with the specific purpose of making genuine traditional flamenco available to the public.

Subsequently, many more sprang up throughout the country and proved to be just as popular as the *cafés cantantes* had been in the second half of the nineteenth century. The irony once again, of course, was that the kind of venue which had led to the decline of flamenco was now the instrument of its salvation, but, in the event, the *tablao*s had a negative as well as a positive effect, as we shall soon see.

In addition, flamenco festivals began to take place on a regular basis, reminiscent of the Granada Festival of 'Deep Song' in 1922. The First National Festival of 'Deep Song' in Córdoba in 1956 was one outstanding example. Serious studies of flamenco appeared in the form of articles and books. At the end of the Spanish Civil War in 1939 flamenco as a serious art had all but disappeared. Now, fifteen years or so later, it flourished again in a startling way – proof, no doubt, not only of its enduring appeal but also of how deeply rooted it is in the Spanish psyche.

The growth of the *tablao*s nevertheless exposed flamenco to the demands and dangers of commercialization no less than the *cafés cantantes* had done previously. The individuals who founded and ran them were, after all, businessmen who in many cases were more concerned with profit than with the art's integrity. As Donn Pohren has suggested, they were more than prepared to encourage a singer to introduce additional flourishes into the performance of a song, as well as to adapt popular songs to flamenco style. Similarly, a female dancer might be persuaded to introduce a gratuitous element of fast and flashy footwork, to move her hips more seductively, to use her facial expressions and arms more provocatively, to incorporate fast and colourful regional dances into her act.

As for a guitarist, he would be asked to focus on faster and more decorative playing and, as in the case of singers and dancers, to adapt popular music to the flamenco guitar. Because they were dependent on the *tablao*s for their livelihood, many flamenco performers felt obliged to compromise, despite their dedication to their art, and they were joined by those whose sights were firmly fixed on stardom and popularity with the general public.

Although the *tablao*s were created with the intention of resuscitating genuine and pure flamenco, commercial pressures threatened to debase it – a danger which Pohren has highlighted in relation to the dancer, Micaela Flores Amaya, better known as La Chunga. Her performance in the early 1950s had been very traditional, characterized by the simplicity and the seriousness appropriate to *baile grande*, and she had worn simple gypsy blouses and skirts and danced barefoot.

Ten years later Pohren saw her dance again, in a *tablao* on the Andalusian coast, and concluded that her performance had been seriously tarnished by the pressures of commercialization. Her earlier simplicity had by now been replaced by a studied artificiality. Her movements and facial expressions, far from being natural, were designed to achieve the greatest effect upon her audience; she used her body and dress in a deliberately seductive manner; and she employed an excessive amount of vulgar footwork. Pohren concluded that commercial pressures 'may possibly succeed in making her just another night club attraction'.

The kind of performance which he describes here is, of course, that experienced by foreign tourists throughout the summer on the Costa del Sol, or indeed by those who participate in group visits to the *tablao*s of the Albaicín or the Sacromonte in Granada. Superficially exciting it may be; true and inspired flamenco it is not.

One of the key figures in the flamenco renaissance was Antonio Mairena. Born of gypsy parents in 1909 in the village of Mairena del Alcor, near Seville, Mairena sang as a boy in the family smithy – what more authentic background could he have had? – and found his inspiration in many of the great flamenco singers of his childhood. He began his professional career at the age of twenty and in due course appeared with many of the greatest performers: the singers Torre, Pavón La Niña de los Peines; the dancer La Macarrona; and the guitarist Javier Molina. Based for the most part in Seville, he also performed in Madrid, in particular at establishments owned by Pastora Imperio, and at one time was

Antonio Mairena, upholder of the flamenco traditions

the lead singer in Antonio's world-famous flamenco company. In 1962 he was awarded the prestigious Golden Key at the Third National Festival of 'Deep Song' in Córdoba.

Mairena's part in the flamenco renaissance was, firstly, that of a singer, and, secondly, that of an educator. As a singer of the purer forms of flamenco song, he was responsible for rescuing from virtual oblivion many of the traditional songs - *tonás, siguiriyas, livianas* - and for breathing new life into them in his performances. Furthermore, he was able through recordings to transmit them to future generations. Through his participation in the organization of important flamenco festivals, he brought together some of the great singers and dancers of the past, reminding younger audiences of what flamenco should be. And finally, through his writings he was able to inform his readers of the history and evolution of flamenco, and of the different kinds of song which were part of it, all of this discussed and explained within the context of a deep knowledge of the subject.

Fidelity to the old forms of flamenco song has, nevertheless, led certain critics to assert that Mairena's singing lacked creativity and genuine emotion and that, in turning his back on innovation, he failed to take flamenco forward. His response to such a charge has been quite clear: 'Flamenco song is there and one has to record it as it is... I do not wish to go beyond that, because in the future artists and aficionados will ask why I recorded something that lies outside the rules of flamenco song, and why I did something that, as an artist, I had no right to do...'

As for the presence or absence of strong emotion in Mairena's singing, opinion has been markedly divided. Some have suggested that he was too intellectual and impersonal to experience true *duende*. In contrast, Juan Talega, a fine flamenco singer in his own right, stated that, with the exception of Torre, Mairena was the best flamenco singer he had ever heard. The division of opinion is explained in part, perhaps, by the fact that Mairena's favourite performance venues were not the theatres but the *juergas*, where his singing would have been less public and the occasions on which he was truly inspired known to fewer people. Whatever the case, Mairena

The singer known as 'Chocolate' (Antonio Nuñez Montoya)

continued and achieved in no small measure the task which de Falla, Lorca and others had set themselves many years earlier in the Granada Festival of 'Deep Song' in 1922.

Manolo Caracol, who, as Manolito Ortega, was one of the prizewinners of that competition, was also part of the flamenco renaissance. Born in 1909 in Triana, the heart of pure flamenco, Caracol was a much more volatile character than Mairena but at his best a magnificent singer, highly reminiscent of the old-style gypsy *cantaores*. As Fernando Quiñones observes, his voice was genuinely *afillá*:

> ...very few voices can have equalled Caracol's from the very
> beginning of flamenco, and certainly none of all those that I have
> listened to...That dark timbre, that roughness, that broken and
> dramatic register in the voice of Manolo Caracol, that Caruso of the
> caves, as it were, seem to capture with incomparable accuracy and
> intensity the socially disrupted world of the Andalusian-gypsy race
> and the suffering of the Andalusian people throughout the
> centuries...

Manolo Caracol, one of the influential singers in the flamenco revival of the twentieth century

Depending on how he felt at a particular moment and on the degree of inspiration which consumed him, he was as capable of scaling the heights of flamenco perfection as of plunging into the depths of mediocrity. Those heights were often achieved in the many *juerga*s in which he took part and often organized at great expense, as well as on his records of *cante grande*.

Three other male singers can be considered in the same context. Antonio Fernández Díaz, better known as Fosforito, was born in Puente Genil in 1932, and, like Mairena, idolized the older forms of flamenco song. Even though he was part of the touring flamenco circuit, he succeeded in preserving his artistic integrity and has been compared with Mairena in both the quality of his singing and his missionary zeal. Another great singer, Antonio Nuñez, known as Chocolate, was born in Jerez in 1931 of gypsy parents, and resembled both Torre and Caracol in the sense that he was a largely instinctive singer. In his own words, 'The Cante will always be a mystery. I realize this when on many occasions, when I am singing, I don't know what it is that is happening in my body.' The same can be said of Fernando Fernández Monje, who possessed the impressive nickname Terremoto de Jerez (Earthquake from Jerez). Born in Jerez in 1934, he had a typical gypsy voice, a *voz afillá*. He was, of course, of true gypsy origin and, like Caracol, could produce as many wonderful as abysmal performances, depending on his mood. According to the flamenco guitarist, Manuel Morao, 'When he was inspired and had that... that... that

light, and we don't know what it is, he could then produce something brilliant, something extraordinary'. His rather childlike nature, which in part explains the intuitive cast of his singing, was revealed on one occasion when, having been awarded an important prize, he demanded that it be much bigger, 'like Real Madrid's European Cup'.

If these singers were involved not only in flamenco's renaissance but also in the regeneration of the older forms of flamenco song, they were followed by others who changed this pattern, in particular José Monje Cruz, better known as Camarón de la Isla, and Enrique Morente. Born in 1950 in La Isla de San Fernando, Cádiz, Camarón grew up surrounded by flamenco tradition. His mother was a fine singer; he was able at first hand to listen to the old flamenco singers; and his family was always close to that of the important female singer La Perla de Cádiz. Having learned his art from the best singers of the time, he had great respect for the traditional forms of flamenco song. Nevertheless, he adapted his singing to more modern forms and softened his style, rather as Chacón had done before him, thereby creating a bridge between the old and the new. The consequence was that Camarón achieved enormous popularity and became a legend in his lifetime. It has been said that many who attended his performances – gypsies, non-gypsies, Japanese, young and old – did so simply to see and hear Camarón, without afterwards wishing to listen to any other performer. Like many flamenco singers before him, he died young – at forty-two – and from the effects of alcohol and drugs, so frequently used by flamenco singers in their efforts to achieve a special performance. His death and funeral attracted the kind of attention generally accorded to a pop-star – a sufficient indication of his reputation.

Enrique Morente, born in Granada in 1942, is a more controversial figure. Like Camarón, he was exposed at a young age to the pure forms of flamenco song, evidence of which is to be found in an early recording, *Cantes antiguos del flamenco* (*Ancient Songs of Flamenco*). Subsequently, however, for reasons which include both boredom with the status quo and a desire to explore new possibilities, he has gone in a different direction, arguing that, if it is not to die of stagnation, pure flamenco must move on. Hence he has adapted the work of such poets as Antonio Machado, Miguel Hernández, and Lorca to the style of flamenco song and, although not a trained musician, has written music for television, cinema and theatre. Particular works include an adaptation for flamenco performance of selected episodes from Cervantes's *Don Quixote*; *Fantasía cante jondo para una misa flamenca* (*Fantasy of Deep Song for a Flamenco Mass*); and *Concierto de cante jondo para voz y orquesta* (*Concerto of Deep Song for Voice and Orchestra*). Needless to say, supporters of traditional flamenco are appalled by such experiments. Donn Pohren has suggested that if

OPPOSITE,
Camarón de la Isla
(José Monje Cruz),
who achieved pop
star adulation

Enrique Morente
(above) stands for a
more modern
approach
to flamenco

Fernanda de Utrera
who, with her sister
Bernarda, ranks
among the top
female flamenco
singers of today

Morente's innovative work makes him 'a hero to a hip Madrid group of young aficionados, also bored with traditional flamenco', it has also presented him as a 'ridiculous figure to most of Andalusia'. On the other hand, Angel Alvarez Caballero, recognizing how difficult it is for the older generation to accept new ideas, pays tribute to Morente when he observes that 'one recognizes bit by bit the enormous merit of his singular work'. The debate clearly continues.

Although female singers of the past fifty years have, predictably, been fewer in number than the men, some of them have been, and continue to be, outstanding. One of the most prominent is Antonia Gilabert Vargas, known as La Perla de Cádiz. As her name implies, she was born in Cádiz, in 1925, and is considered by many to be the best female singer of this period. As much at home in the serious forms of flamenco song, such as the *siguiriya*, as in the lighter forms, she has a voice which is firm, brilliant and flexible, and is in some ways reminiscent of La Niña de los Peines, a comparison which points to her true artistic stature.

Two others are sisters, Fernanda and Bernarda de Utrera, born in 1923 and 1927, who represent the older flamenco forms. Francisca Méndez Garrido, born in Jerez in 1934 and better known as La Paquera de Jerez, is a particularly powerful singer of *bulerías*. Of the younger generation, Carmen Linares is regarded by many as perhaps the best. Born in the mining town of Linares, in Jaén, in 1951, she has made a serious study of all the forms of flamenco song, from the *siguiriyas* and the *soleares* to the *malagueñas* and the *fandangos*. Her preference for the older types of flamenco song clearly distinguishes her from someone like Enrique Morente and suggests perhaps that female singers are more traditional.

During the last fifty years, as in earlier times, flamenco dance has been largely dominated by women, much as flamenco song has by men. They include Rosita Durán, Lucerito Tena, Luisa Maravilla, Micaela Flores Amaya, La Chunga, Cristina Hoyos, Blanca del Rey, Manuela Vargas, Merche Esmeralda, and Manuela Carrasco. In the history of flamenco dance, as we have seen, there was a gradual transition from concentration on the movements of the hands, arms and upper body to an increased emphasis on footwork, and most dancers in the modern period have been proficient in both. Rosita Durán, born in 1920, was the leading dancer in the famous La Zambra *tablao* in Madrid in the 1950s and '60s. A firm believer in the traditional aspects of flamenco dance, she was particularly good in the use of the hands and upper body, but her footwork, when required, was also effective. If anything, the footwork of Lucerito Tena, born in1936 in Mexico, was even stronger and more intricate, but she too was highly skilled in the classic aspects of the dance. More traditional than both, however, was Luisa Maravilla, who was born in Madrid in 1939. She favoured the slower, more serious dances – those based on the *siguiriya* and the *soleá* – and therefore emphasized the slow expressive movements of the hands and arms. It is interesting to note that for this very reason her style was not well suited to the *tablao*s, where the dancing is usually faster and more frenzied. Maravilla therefore preferred to dance in more authentic locations – at gypsy festivals, for example – where a more spontaneous and expressive kind of flamenco dance could be performed to a more appreciative audience.

The best-known female dancer of the last thirty years or so is probably Cristina Hoyos, who was born in Seville in 1946. After coming to prominence as a teenager and dancing at the Spanish Pavilion at the World's Fair in New York in 1964, she perfected her art in the most important *tablao*s throughout Spain, and then in

Cristina Hoyos, who combines the traditional and the modern in her dancing, seen in the film of Manuel de Falla's *El amor brujo*, directed by Carlos Saura

Cristina Hoyos in the stage version of Lorca's *Blood Wedding* by the Antonio Gades Company

1969 became the principal dancer in the company of Antonio Gades, with whom she would be associated in various important projects for the next twenty years. In 1974 she played the part of the Bride, opposite Gades's Bridegroom, in the flamenco-dance stage version of Lorca's *Blood Wedding* (*Bodas de sangre*). In 1981 it was made into the well-known film directed by Carlos Saura. Two years later Saura made his even better-known film, *Carmen*, with Laura del Sol in the title role and Cristina Hoyos playing the part of the company's dance teacher. And in 1985 she appeared in the final film of the Saura-Gades dance trilogy, *Love the Magician* (*El amor brujo*), based on the ballet by de Falla.

The collaboration with Antonio Gades has not, however, prevented her from doing other work. During the 1970s she performed with her own company in Europe and Japan. In the mid-1980s she presented and danced in her own version of *Carmen*, set up another company in 1988 and appeared in several films. In 1989 she danced in and, with Manolo Marín, choreographed *Flamenco Dreams* (*Sueños flamencos*), which opened in Paris and subsequently visited many capital cities, including London.

Another important year was 1992, when she not only presented *Yerma and the Flamenco Spirit* (*Yerma y lo flamenco*) at Expo '92 in Seville but also danced at the opening and closing ceremonies of the Olympic Games in Barcelona. Hoyos combines the old and the new. Taught by Seville's leading flamenco dance teacher, Enrique el Cojo, who favoured the movements of hands, arms and upper body, she evokes in her art the style of the *cafés cantantes*, but her intricate and often dramatic footwork is much more modern. It has been said of her that she 'pays homage to popular tradition whilst offering us a taste of the contemporary'.

This melding of past and present is also true of the other leading female dancers. Blanca del Rey, born in 1949 in Córdoba, combines traditional elements with innovation and has contributed greatly to the survival of much that is pure in flamenco dance. Manuela Vargas, born in Seville in 1941 of gypsy parents, was taught, like Hoyos, by Enrique el Cojo. Initially outstanding in the performance of a fiery *rumba*, she later added other dances to her repertoire and toured many countries with her own company. Nine years younger but also born in Seville, Merche Esmeralda began dancing in the late 1960s. Her style is highly traditional, though over the years she has also embraced non-flamenco dance styles and performed with the Spanish National Ballet. The youngest dancer of this group, Manuela Carrasco, could not have a more authentic background. Born in 1958 in the Sevillian district of Triana, she began her career in the aptly named *tablao* El Jaleo in Torremolinos and thereafter became a highly acclaimed performer throughout Spain. She so impressed the great flamenco singer Caracol that he invited her to dance at his *tablao* in Madrid, Los Canasteros. More recently she has appeared in two films directed by Carlos Saura, *Sevillanas* and *Flamenco*, and has also toured many countries in flamenco stage shows. The dancer Antonio calls her 'a reincarnation of ancestral gypsy women'.

Of the male dancers of the last forty years, the best known is undoubtedly Antonio Gades, his fame outside Spain linked in no small measure to his star-

Cristina Hoyos and her company in her staging of Lorca's *Yerma*

ring roles in Saura's films. Born in Elda, Alicante, in 1936, he was spotted at the age of fifteen by Pilar López, sister of La Argentinita, who invited him to join her company. During the following nine years he acquired a knowledge of flamenco, regional Spanish dance and classical ballet and, when he finally left the Pilar López company he set up the group which would eventually become the Ballet Antonio Gades. Determined to rid flamenco of the flamboyance and flashiness which he considered detrimental, he resolved to achieve a greater simplicity, a quality much to the fore in his stage version of *Blood Wedding*. It was a production which served to confirm his international reputation, and in 1978, three years after the death of Franco, Gades was invited by the new democratic regime to direct the Spanish National Ballet. When he was removed from this position three years later, he began the partnership with Saura. In addition, he toured world-wide his own stage version of *Carmen* and also created *Fuego* (*Fire*), a free version of *Love the Magician*. In 1994, once more with his own company, he created *Fuente Ovejuna*, his dance version of Lope de Vega's famous seventeenth-century play. Gades has a complete mastery of flamenco forms and, in the course of a long career, has succeeded in achieving in his performance an unvarnished purity that characterizes flamenco at its finest and most authentic with the strength and virility which have always been the essence of the male flamenco dancer.

Among contemporary dancers the rising star is considered by many to be Joaquín Cortés, who at thirty is a good deal younger than Gades. Of his outstanding ability there is no doubt, as is shown by his performances in two recent films: Pedro Almodóvar's *The Flower of My Secret* (*La flor de mi secreto*), and Saura's *Flamenco* in which he delivers a powerful *farruca*. Cortés, however,

The dancer Antonio Gades and the film director Carlos Saura, with whom he has often worked

A scene from Saura's film version of *Blood Wedding*

has been attracted to popular culture of various kinds from an early age. When he was fourteen or so, he performed flamenco-flavoured pop songs on Spanish television, and nowadays the influence of popular genres is increasingly evident in his stage shows. Cortés has persistently defended this aspect of his work in the name of innovation, but he has been much criticized as well.

Placing flamenco on stage and in the cinema have raised concerns about authenticity. To cite once example, Madeleine Claus has observed that the stage shows presented by Gades are characterized by 'impeccable staging and the almost scientifically geometric precision of his choreography', but concludes that 'flamenco – the lonely, personal, spontaneous expression of an artist – is lost in the telling...' They are, in short, performances distinguished by much calculation and little heart. Gades's own assessment of the qualities most central to his stage-version and his film of *Carmen* is quite different:

> In the film and in the stage-version, our dance has strength, it is truly alive. It is not an academic dance in which what is seen is almost an analysis, a technique... It is not a dance which is cold, but the manifestation of what certain human beings feel who through the medium of dance express a state of mind...

Indeed, he draws a clear distinction between classical dance, which requires good looks and a well-honed physique, and the dancers in his own company,

Two scenes from
Carlos Saura's film
Carmen, which starred
Antonio Gades and
Cristina Hoyos

who place their emphasis very firmly on individuality and the expression of the inner self rather than on pure technique: 'The fat ones dance, the bald ones, the handsome ones, the old ones, all have the right to dance... Everyone has the right to dance. And isn't that to make technique human?'

As for his own performance, Gades describes his total identification with dance and his expression through it of his inner self as 'the medium which has offered me the possibility of self-expression, which has provided me with the same degree of expression as a painter has with his paint...' Here he contradicts the suggestion that in his stage shows and films the 'personal, spontaneous expression of an artist' is somehow lost. He rejects too the notion that he has deliberately geared performances towards a more popular audience: 'On stage I have never made concessions. If I occasionally have..., I can honestly say that I was not aware that I was doing so...'

Certainly there can be no doubt of the flamenco character of the Gades-Saura film, *Carmen*. In its making, both creators were fired by the desire to place the story in a Spanish setting in general and in the context of flamenco in particular. Saura considered Bizet's treatment of Mérimée's story to have toned down its earthiness, violence and sensuality in order to accommodate the tastes of a bourgeois Parisian audience, while his music, though very attractive, was far from being genuinely Spanish. The two therefore set out to restore the story's earthiness and to emphasize its Spanish character through the presence of flamenco elements – a process which is very evident in an early sequence. As Antonio, the artistic director of a Spanish dance company, listens to a tape-recording of the well-known *seguidilla* from Act One – Carmen flirting with Don José after her arrest – he requests that the music be adapted for flamenco performance. Voice and orchestra are therefore replaced by guitar, dance and clapping, and the rhythm of Bizet's music, which is too slow for flamenco, is quickened to that of *bulerías*. Later, flamenco becomes the cornerstone of sequence after sequence.

Despite the preponderance of flamenco elements in the film, the question still remains: do they possess the true spirit of flamenco, or are they rehearsed and choreographed to the point of cold precision? In this respect, Gades's contentions about expressing through the medium of dance that which lies within are triumphantly vindicated. In a solo dance, the *farruca* which he performs for Carmen, he expresses through the character of Antonio all that he feels within himself, and does so as solo flamenco dancers have done throughout the centuries – in strong, simple and austere movement, without any kind of musical accompaniment. The same is true of the more complex dance sequences involving many dancers, which are examples of meticulous choreography that yet expresses at every stage the many shades of love, hate,

Suite flamenca:
Cristina Hoyos and
Antonio Gades

jealousy and anguish that have always been at the heart of flamenco. In short, technique is merely the servant of the passion which runs so vibrantly through the story; and if it is suggested that flamenco has here been elevated to high art, which is far removed from what it once was, it can also be argued that this is high art ablaze with emotion, uniting performer and audience as did flamenco of old. Indeed, in the stage-version of *Carmen* presented by the Compañía Antonio Gades at the Sadler's Wells Theatre in London in 1996 and at the Peacock Theatre in 1997, the enthusiasm of the audience was such that individuals shouted their encouragement and approval, creating in that sense the heady atmosphere of a traditional *juerga*, even if the London audience was not intoxicated in quite the same way. Though the show was performed night after night, repeated performance did not mean – and need not mean – that, within the overall structure and within a particular dance, a dancer could not introduce innovation and spontaneity. Any suggestion that the passion displayed by the old-time flamenco singers and dancers was not present here is quite misguided.

The same can be said of the shows performed by other flamenco companies in recent years, different as they may have been. Consider, for example, *Flamenco Dreams,* presented by the Ballet Cristina Hoyos. The programme consisted not of a story, as in the case of *Carmen,* but of a series of dances which covered all three categories of *baile grande, intermedio* and *chico.* Performed either by Cristina Hoyos individually or by members of the company, a *siguiriya, farruca, bambera, tango, alegría, taranto, soleá* and *bulería* all suggested the various moods of flamenco.

In contrast, the first half of *Flamenco Heart (Corazón flamenco)*, performed in many countries in the mid-1990s and directed by Francisco Sánchez, was narrative based. The story, entitled *St James's Night (Noche de Santiago)*, involved a husband, his wife and a male gypsy, bringing to mind *Blood Wedding*, in which a wife runs off with her former lover and is hunted down by her wronged husband. Francisco Sánchez, who has worked extensively with the flamenco group Cumbre flamenca, has observed that in staging a story he wished to show that the possibilities of flamenco are narrative as well as expressive, thereby expanding the traditional form.

On the other hand, the second half of the programme, called *The Deepest* (*Lo más hondo*), emphasized the traditional dance, beginning, for example, with the performance of a *siguiriya* by Manuela Carrasco, who later in the programme also danced a *soleá*. These two examples of the slower and essentially serious flamenco dances contrasted markedly with the exciting *bulerías* finale, danced by the whole company. In short, *Flamenco Heart* balanced the traditional with experiment and innovation characteristic of modern flamenco, at the same time revealing the influence of the theatre.

Manuela Carrasco and her daughter on the patio of their house in Seville

A similar mix is to be found in the flamenco shows presented by Paco Peña, an influential figure in recent times. Born in Córdoba in 1942, he began playing the guitar professionally at around twelve years of age, largely as an accompanist, and turned soloist in the early 1960s.

In 1970 he formed the Paco Peña Flamenco Company, which he has since taken all over the world. During the last decade the company has presented two shows – *Art and Passion* (*Arte y Pasión*) and *Gypsy Muse* (*Musa gitana*) –

Angel Muñoz, star of the Paco Peña company, 1998

Paco Peña and his company in London in *Art and Passion*, 1998

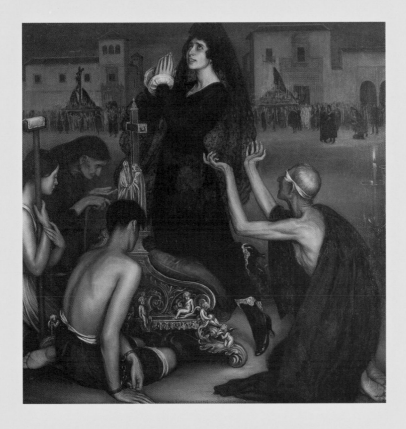

which illustrated very clearly both traditional and experimental elements. In *Art and Passion* the range of traditional flamenco was much in evidence. A *martinete* and a *soleá* were performed by two male dancers and accompanied by a singer; two more serious dances, a *tientos* and a *zapateado*, were performed by three dancers and one respectively; a *granaina* (*cante intermedio*) was sung by a female singer; and in the programme's second half a series of lighter and more exuberant dances – *bulerías, tangos*, a *garrotín* – were dazzlingly presented by the whole company.

Gypsy Muse, on the other hand, was significantly different. Each dance followed on from a slide-projection of a painting by the Cordoban artist Julio Romero de Torres (1874-1930). The painting entitled *Saeta*, for example, depicted the figures who participate in the Holy Week processions in Andalusia, and its projection therefore gave way to the performance of a *saeta* itself, powerfully sung and accompanied by drums, trumpets and dancers. In contrast, the projection of the painting *Oranges and Lemons* (*Naranjas y limones*) led to the dancing of *bulerías* at a frenzied pace. Throughout the programme the serious and the lighter forms of flamenco, as well as the elements of song, dance and guitar, were judiciously balanced, allowing the performers every opportunity to demonstrate their skill. Above all, *Gypsy Muse* made room for individual expression and, by introducing a series of paintings as catalyst, gave the show a novel twist.

A painting by Julio Romero de Torres, *Saeta*, used in the Paco Peña staging of *Gypsy Muse*, 1999

The integrity of these outstanding artists distinguished these shows from those of the 1920s and '30s in which flamenco was diminished by the introduction of popular, non-flamenco elements. The threat returns, however, in the performances of Joaquín Cortés. His most recent flamenco show, *Gypsy Passion* (*Pasión gitana*), began with Cortés making his entrance not from the wings but via the central aisle of the auditorium. His hair was long, dark and flowing, his face illuminated by a beam of golden light; he wore a black sarong. It was the entrance of a pop star – indeed, there were squeals from the younger members of the audience – and reminiscent too of the gaudily orchestrated entrances into the ring of boxers in a championship fight. In the light of such ballyhoo, we can well imagine the disgust of great flamenco dancers past, in Lorca's phrase, their 'ancient knives/trembling beneath the dust'. As for Cortes's dance performance, it received short shrift from the critics. Their comments on his limited technique were undoubtedly more relevant to this particular show than to his real ability, but both his performance and the stage-presentation in general were clear evidence of an attempt to combine flamenco and show business: lighting effects, the use of two video screens

Joaquín Cortés, a flamboyant, popular star of the day, in *Gypsy Passion*, 1997

echoing the events on stage, an amplified band, and costumes more suited to the fashion catwalk. One of the critics observed,

Three young flamenco guitarists of the group Calle Nueva in Seville

> When you see and hear a really great flamenco show, the performers become almost impersonal conductors of rhythm and emotion. They plug into a history, a culture much larger than themselves. The disappointment of *Gypsy Passion* is that even with its high-tech trappings it doesn't add up to a powerful event. The emotion is too glibly manufactured, the climaxes too stage-managed and the images too facile...Cortés may sell out wherever he dances, but it is a triumph of hype over experience.

Given such comments, it is not surprising to discover that Cortés is both dismissive of and uninterested in the great dancers of the past and the present. The former, especially in the early days of flamenco, were paid very little. They performed for their suppers and, of course, for their art. Today the adverse influence of money is to be seen everywhere, in show-business as in sport, and it is no respecter of integrity. The point is surely illustrated by Cortés's participation in the 1999 Oscars ceremony, where he danced to the music of the film *Saving Private Ryan*!

Traditionally in the background, flamenco guitarists risk being overlooked. The best known today is undoubtedly Paco de Lucía, who was born in Algeciras in 1947. His outstanding talent was evident when, at the age of fourteen, he was awarded the first prize for amateur guitarists at the Jerez de la Frontera flamenco contest. Subsequently, the family – his father was his teacher – moved to Madrid and Paco quickly made his name as a professional, not least as the result of the recordings which he made with the singer Camarón when he was barely out of his teens. But if these recordings reveal his enormous talent as an accompanist of traditional flamenco song, much of his later work has involved experiment with other kinds of music, in particular jazz and Brazilian music, which he has adapted to flamenco styles. He is one of those artists who has attempted to expand the boundaries of flamenco, but always with a sense of integrity, refusing to pander to commercial considerations.

Older than Paco de Lucía but equally eminent are Melchor de Marchena, born in 1913 in a town near Seville, and Agustín Castellón, better known as Sabicas, who was born in Pamplona in the same year. The great difference between them illustrates some of the points made earlier. Melchor de Marchena, though a virtuoso of the guitar, brought to his playing an intensity of emotion reminiscent of that of Caracol in his singing of a *siguiriya,* and he was indeed Caracol's accompanist for many years at Los Canasteros in Madrid. He was a lover of the old traditions. Sabicas, in contrast, has been described as the maestro of the concert-hall flamenco guitarists. Featured as a solo guitarist with several flamenco companies before the Civil War, he then left Spain and lived in Mexico City before moving on to New York in 1957, finally returning to his native country after thirty years. His status as a guitar virtuoso suggests, of course, that his mastery of the techniques of the flamenco guitar is complete, but he is also a great accompanist, as his many recordings prove. It is felt by some, however, that his technical skill – an essential requirement in a concert-hall performer – deprives his playing of the raw emotion and inspiration evident in the performance of Melchor de Marchena.

The outreach explored by Paco de Lucía for the last fifteen years or so characterizes the movement known as New Flamenco. Indeed, the recordings he made with Camarón around 1981, of which *Como el agua (Like Water)* is one example, seem to have paved the way. During the 1960s and '70s thousands of people, turning their backs on the poverty and high unemployment of Andalusia, flocked to Madrid in search of better times. This migration pulled the focus of flamenco from the south to the centre where their children, the young flamenco musicians of today, have grown up. One of the new groups, La Barbería del Sur, consists of three young gypsies whose families are steeped in traditional flamenco. The guitarist David Amaya is the son of the flamenco dancer, La Tati, a highly accomplished *bailaora,* while his father is the nephew of the legendary Carmen Amaya. It is hardly surprising that, as a child, David Amaya should have been steeped in the traditions of flamenco; but, like many young people, he was also attracted to other forms of music, especially rock,

Paco de Lucía (left)
and Pedro Baca

reggae and jazz. The flamenco played by the group draws, therefore, on many kinds of music, and their 1995 album, *Knock Us Down If You Can* (*Túmbanos si puedes*), contains elements of samba, salsa, and heavy metal, though at the same time there are flamenco *tangos*, a *bulerías*, and a Charlie Parker number adapted to flamenco style.

Another leading flamenco group, Ketama, consists of four young men, all Madrid-born and bred, whose families originate in Granada and Jerez. Like the musicians of La Barbería del Sur, the members of the group have a classic flamenco background, but their instruments include electric guitar, synthesizers and drums; their music, though permeated by the rhythms of flamenco, has strong elements of pop, rock, reggae and Latin American. Lead vocalist Antonio Carmona sings about being a young gypsy in the big city, enjoying life

Sara Baras in her 1999
touring show

and falling in love – narratives that reflect the modern world of night-clubs and video games, a world away from the roadside inns and taverns of Andalusia. Ketama has also collaborated with other musicians, thereby mixing styles. In 1988, for example, the group joined up with Toumani Diabate, an expert performer on the 'kora' (an eight-string African harp), and with Danny Thompson, a British acoustic bass player. The album *Songhai* was the result of their collaboration.

Other contemporary groups also reveal a mixture of styles. Amalgama combines flamenco, jazz and Indian music and includes a flamenco and an Indian female singer. Indian instruments are used, as well as flute and guitar. Jazz pianist Chano Domínguez mixes jazz, rock and flamenco rhythms and, with guitar, acoustic bass and percussion accompaniment, seeks to imitate on the piano the sounds and technique of the flamenco guitar. In contrast, Radio Tarifa is the brainchild of Faín Dueñas, an electric guitarist who has immersed himself in both African and Arabic percussion and also mastered the techniques of Arabic, Moroccan and Turkish stringed instruments. Rather different again are Willi Giménez and Chanela, a group of six Giménez brothers who mix flamenco, Caribbean music and American rhythm and blues, thereby creating a style known as rumba funky. Yet another group, Pata Negra, formed by two brothers from Seville, creates an amalgam of flamenco, rock and blues.

These styles all appear at first to be both innovative and imaginative, and this new kind of flamenco is usually described as moving with the times. Yet the question arises: moving towards what? Listening to it leaves the impression that this music is novel, clever and, in its way, attractive. But it also strikes many people as lacking in true emotional power. The comparison which springs to mind is that between traditional jazz and the modern jazz of twenty years ago – the latter intricate, the former raw and emotional. The instruments employed by some of these New Flamenco groups -– flute, harp, bass, harmonium – inevitably lead to a soft sound, while the rhythms of samba and salsa, flowing and quick-moving, are very different from those of pure flamenco. The singers, too, pale into insignificance in comparison with the singers of true flamenco, who still seek to keep the authentic tradition alive.

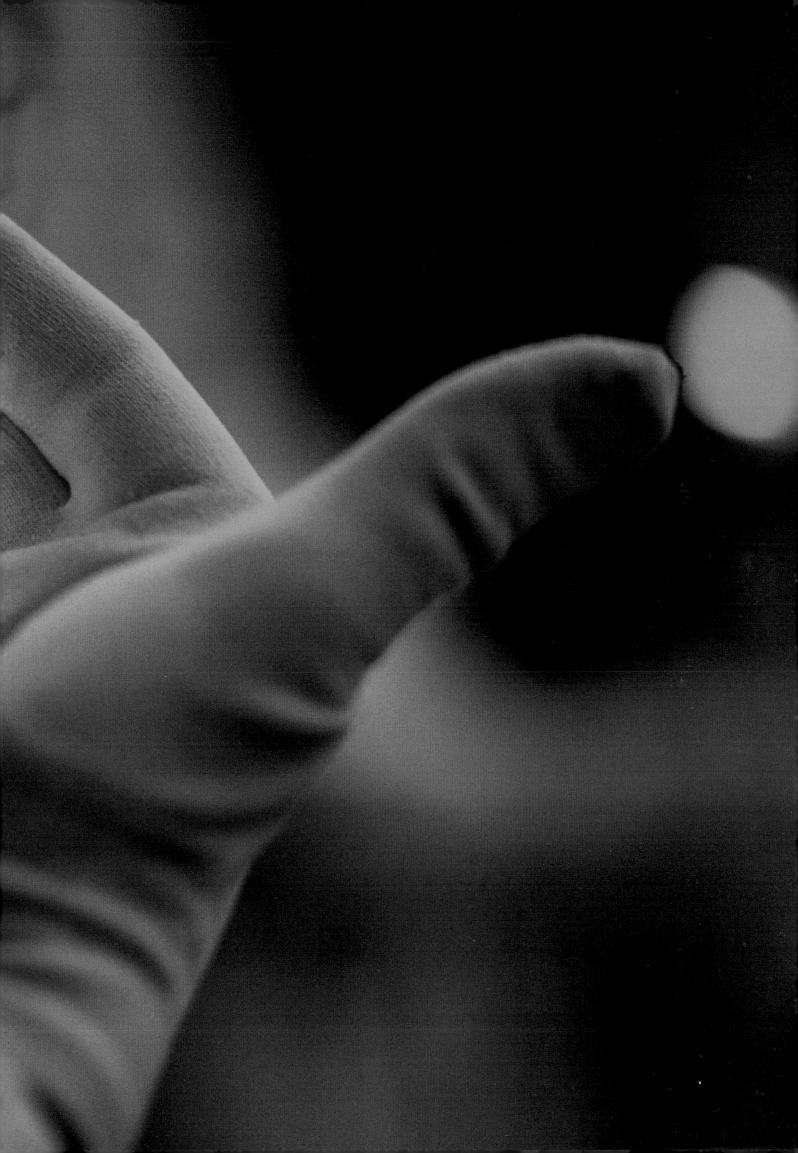

CHAPTER 4
Flamenco in its broader context

HOLY WEEK in Seville. Evening. Along one of its main streets the procession advances slowly. Barefooted penitents carry on aching shoulders the large, heavy, and lavishly decorated platforms on which are displayed sculpted images of the Virgin or the crucified Christ. Behind the penitents the silent worshippers make their way, all of them wearing cloaks and tall, pointed hoods, and carrying lighted candles in their hands. Heavy drumbeats accompany the snail-like pace, stopping when the penitents stop to gather strength and catch their breath. As they get under way once more, the drums thunder, the crowd applauds in the packed streets, and raucous trumpets pierce the air. In a while they stop again, and from a balcony a flamenco singer addresses an anguished lament, a *saeta*, to the image of the Virgin:

La Virgen de la Esperanza, a seventeenth-century figure by an unknown artist, which is carried in the Holy Week procession in Seville

Toítas las mares tienen penas,	*All mothers have sorrows,*
pero la tuya es la mayor	*But yours is the greatest*
porque delante llevas a tu	*Because you have before you your*
[Hijo amante,	*[beloved Son,*
amarraíto de pies y manos,	*His feet and hands tied,*
como si fuera un traidor.	*As if he were a traitor.*

Flamenco in a religious context? The foreign visitor might well be surprised, and surprised too to learn of the close connection between flamenco, religion and the bullfight, and of Andalusia's links with the ancient world.

Consider first the links between flamenco and religion. During the seventeenth and eighteenth centuries, as Timothy Mitchell has pointed out, the funeral processions of the wealthy were often accompanied by female singers called *endecheras* or *plañideras* ('wailers') who were specialists in the art of singing *endechas*, songs of grieving and lamentation sung in a highly emotional manner, which in turn had a strong effect on the mourners themselves. These songs, or at least the style in which they were sung, are often considered to have been the antecedent of the *siguiriya*, the most emotional type of flamenco song. The word *playera*, which derives from *plañidera*, was at one point in flamenco's evolution a synonym for *siguiriya*, which therefore points to a

Pastora Pavón
singing a *saeta*
from her balcony

connection between a Christian ritual -- in this instance a funeral with its attendant Christian ceremonies -- and one of the most important types of flamenco song.

The *saeta*, which came to be sung in the Holy Week processions, is even more clearly rooted in religion. One possibility is that it was originally a chant, strongly influenced by the liturgical chant, which was intoned during the Holy Week celebrations. Another suggestion is that it stemmed from a Moorish *azan*, a muezzin or priest's call of the faithful to prayers. After the defeat of the Moors in 1492, its sounds seem to have disappeared but surfaced again when Moors were burned at the stake for religious offences, and grieving mothers cried out for their condemned sons. A third theory is that it was sung by Jews who wished to remove all doubts about their conversion to Christianity and who therefore insisted, as genuine believers, on taking part in the Holy Week processions. In each case, the religious origin of the *saeta* is undeniable.

From the seventeenth century, brotherhoods known as *cofradías* were involved in the organization of the Holy Week processions throughout Andalusia. When one stopped outside a prison, the prisoners sang an early form of *saeta* to the figures of the Virgin and the crucified Christ, thereby venting their feelings of guilt and remorse, and evoking intense feelings in the watching crowd. Later still, the role of the prisoner was assumed by professional singers, *saeteros*, and by the late nineteenth century the *saeta*s were certainly being sung by some of the most famous flamenco singers, including the legendary Enrique el Mellizo, who was born in Cádiz in 1848. During the Holy Week processions he and his children – two sons and a daughter – would position themselves on the balconies of his house on the corner of a street in Cádiz. When the procession arrived, the four of them sang *saeta*s, halting the march for a considerable time and stirring the spectators to displays of great emotion.

If the involvement of the gypsies in the events of Holy Week appears to run counter to their general lack of interest in orthodox religion, their identification with the Crucifixion is quite easily explained. For them Christ is a fellow-sufferer, cruelly persecuted and abused as they have been throughout their history. Mary, grieving for her son, embodies the sorrow of many a gypsy mother who weeps for a son languishing in prison or in hiding from the authorities. It was therefore fitting that the *saeta* should have been sung so often in the form of the *siguiriya*, the kind of flamenco song most suited to the expression of powerful emotion.

In certain parts of Andalusia the older forms of the *saeta* are still sung. In Arcos de la Frontera, for example, a *saeta* reminiscent in style of Gregorian chant is sung to the accompaniment of fairly primitive wind instruments. In Puente Genil, during Lent rather than Holy Week, the various brotherhoods meet every Sunday and during their meal *saeta*s in the form of a dialogue are recited rather than sung, after which the assembled company makes its way to the Hermitage of Jesus of Nazareth to the accompaniment of more *saeta*s.

Good Friday Procession in Seville, painting by Manuel Cabra, 1862

An illustration
of flamenco singers
by D.F. Lameyer
for Estébanez
Calderón's *Escenas
Andaluzas*, 1847

In Utrera the nuns have their own particular *saeta*s, considered to be both pure and ancient in origin.

In small towns the processions of Holy Week are predictably less ostentatious than those in the larger towns and cities, where one church vies with another to field the most lavish float, and where the presence of vast crowds can be due as much to curiosity as to devotion. Even in the smaller processions the *saeta* is much in evidence and religious feeling profound. In this respect flamenco is, indeed, part of that intense spirituality which at points in Spanish history has inspired such individuals as Saint Teresa and Saint John of the Cross, also expressed in the flame-like figures in the paintings of El Greco.

Yet sustaining this link between religion and flamenco becomes difficult because in the course of its subsequent evolution flamenco was most often found where religious associations were notable only by their absence: at inns and taverns, where liquor flowed freely, often among people of questionable repute. But the powerful mix of alcohol, music and the camaraderie of shared emotion surely created an atmosphere akin to religious trance or communion – a state in which members of the audience identified not only with the singer but also with each other. Indeed, in the eyes of many, the flamenco singer became a kind of god, as Felix Grande has observed of his own reaction when he attending a performance by Manolo Caracol in Cádiz in 1969: 'In one of those cries... I can hear a voice which is full of trembling and which whispers: "He is a god..."'

In a sense the *cantaor,* singing of black fate, of the wretched nature of human existence, of the misery of unrequited love, takes upon himself the emotional burden, even the sins of his listeners, and, exposing his own wounds and suffering, becomes a Christ figure, a receptacle for the anguish of his audience, whose release of emotion is both catharsis and expiation.

Moreover, the relationship between singer and audience recalls that between a preacher and his congregation in non-conformist chapels and gospel meetings. Like the flamenco singer, the preacher plays upon the emotions of his listeners, drawing from them cries of 'Halleluja' – in effect, the equivalent of the flamenco audience's '¡Olé!' And singing – or the use of the voice in a way which is very close to singing – plays a major part in a preacher's performance. Rhetorical devices such as emphasis on particular words, exaggerating and drawing them out for effect, repetition, changes of tone and rhythm enable the preacher to arouse his congregation to the point where, as in a flamenco performance, they are so involved that they call out in response to his words, some openly weeping. Consider the following: 'And when I sang "Why did God take her?", the man stood up and came towards me. He was crying, crying, but he gave me such a slap and then he embraced me and cried even more...' Although the passage describes a reaction to the flamenco singing of Pericón de Cádiz, it could easily be applied to emotions evoked at gospel meetings.

Foreign visitors to Spain have also observed in flamenco a quality which is ancient, ritualistic and universal. When attending a 1955 flamenco performance in Triana, H.V. Morton saw a clear connection between this dance and those of ancient civilizations: 'With a swirl of her dusty skirts she had abolished the modern world, and I thought of the Phoenician galleys coming into Gades [Cádiz], of Herod's banqueting hall, of the Greek vases in the British Museum with their dancers...'

Gustave Doré's print of the Holy Week procession

Two early depictions
of dancing girls:
(above) a Syrian lustre
painting on glass
(seventh to eighth
century AD) and a
detail from a Pompeii
wall painting

For Edward Hutton, who had visited the Café de Novedades in Seville thirty years earlier, flamenco dance suggested much more than a visual spectacle:

'It is not a joyful thing at all, this strange, vivid struggle, in a dance that is like a battle in the soul that has communicated itself to the flesh. It is really a passionate, almost a religious expression of life...'

And when, somewhat later, Vita Sackville-West found herself at a Sevillian gypsy fiesta, she felt that the voice of a female singer 'suggested some primeval sorrow', and that the movement of gypsy dancers was 'so impersonal as to transcend anything trivial or ephemeral in the emotion, and to translate it into eternal terms...'

In suggesting a connection between Andalusia and the ancient world and the way in which flamenco transcends the ages, these visitors to Spain were reaffirming a long-held belief. Andrew Anderson has noted that for the ancients the region known as Tartessus – the name could signify a kingdom, a country, a region, a city or a river, but probably alluded to what is now Andalusia – was to be found at what was for them the most western point of the world. The city of Tartessus, whose existence has been clearly established, must have been close to ancient Gades – modern Cádiz – and could well have been situated in the delta of the river Guadalquivir, in the area between Seville and Huelva. This connection between the old world and the new fascinated many twentieth-century Spanish artists and intellectuals, for it suggested not merely a historical link but also the extent to which the spirit and the values of the ancient world endured in present-day Andalusia. García Lorca, who has evoked the essence of the region more successfully than any other modern Spanish writer, described how, as a child, he became aware of Andalusia's ancient history when, on his father's estate, a plough turned up a Roman mosaic, confirming the region's affinity with an older civilization and in the process providing him with a rich source of inspiration in years to come.

As we have seen, the gypsies of Andalusia were also descended from an ancient civilization. Not only did they have their origins in India; ancient songs and dances were also the true source of flamenco, and Hindu dancers had arrived in Spain as early as 500 BC. In this context it is not surprising that Lorca should have seen the gypsy as the perfect embodiment of Andal- usia itself or that he should have given expression to this view in *Gypsy Ballads*, a volume of poetry published to great acclaim in 1928. In commenting on the significance of the gypsy in the poems, Lorca observed:

> Although it is called Gypsy, the book as a whole is the poem of
> Andalusia, and I have called it Gypsy because the Gypsy is the most
> distinguished, profound and aristocratic element in my country, the

one that most represents its way of being and best preserves the fire,
the blood and the alphabet of Andalusian and universal truth...

He sought, then, to capture in his work the age-old spirit of his homeland,
embodying in the eternal -- not the present-day -- gypsy the anguish, despair
and mythical character of Andalusia throughout its long and varied history.

Flamenco song, or 'deep song' as Lorca liked to call it, was part of the same
process, a point of contact with the ancient world, a bridge connecting it with
the present day. In a lecture entitled '"Deep Song". Primitive Andalusian
Song', which he delivered in February 1922, four months prior to the presentation in Granada of the important Festival of Deep Song, Lorca repeatedly drew
attention to flamenco's ancient roots. 'Deep Song' – the old, pure songs which
belong to *cante grande* – must be sought, he observed, 'in the primitive musical
systems of India, that is to say, in the very first manifestations of song...' To this
he added: 'It comes from distant races, crossing the graveyard of the years and
the fronds of parched winds...' And of the *siguiriya*, the most emotional of the
songs of *cante grande*, he concluded that it was 'the cry of dead generations, a
painful elegy to lost centuries, the moving evocation of love under other
moons and other winds...' Furthermore, 'deep song' is capable of expressing
the deepest and most universal emotions, the 'most infinite gradations of
Sorrow and Pain, placed at the service of the most pure and exact expression...'
In *Poem of Deep Song* (1931), Lorca made the same connections. The great flamenco singer Juan Breva is described, for example, as being like the blind
Homer. A hand which puts out the flame of an oil-lamp is like Medusa, and the
flame itself is an Indian fakir. Lorca also frequently used the word 'millennial'
to describe the ancient nature of many things to be found in twentieth-century
Andalusia. But it must be emphasized that in this respect he was not unique,
for he was voicing a belief shared by many.

The Granada Festival of 'Deep Song', in which both Lorca and the com-
poser de Falla played an important part, was, as we have noted, an attempt to
safeguard and revive the ancient and pure quality of *cante grande*. Though not
the success it might have been, contemporary accounts of it bear witness to
both flamenco's ancient heritage and the stylized, ritualistic nature of its performance. The musicologist and friend of de Falla, J.B. Trend observed that

> The singing suggested once again that primitive Andalusian song is
> a secular counterpart to plain-song; at any rate the melodies of *cante
> jondo* are made of much the same material as some of the Gregorian
> melodies of the Church; while the wailing Ay! or Leli, leli! with which
> many of them began, had a definitely Oriental suggestion. A cold

Sketch by Lorca of the
gypsy Soledad Montoya in
Romancero gitano

Doré's dancing gypsy girl

Cover of Lorca's *Poema del Cante Jondo*, published in 1931

Title page of lecture on 'deep song' (described as 'the primitive Andalusian song') given at the 1922 Granada festival

analysis can give little idea of the musical effect, the passionate exaltation of the singing, the profound tragedy of the words, and the sheer beauty of style of the whole performance. The songs were not curious and interesting survivals from an Oriental past, but living pieces of music charged with every emotion which tradition, memory, surroundings and pure musical beauty could give them...

Flamenco may be usefully considered too in the context of one kind of ancient ritual – Greek tragedy – and the release of emotion associated with it. The Greek theatre at Epidaurus is one of the best preserved and reveals clearly the physical nature of such performance spaces: the acting area consisted of a circle around which the audience sat on steeply tiered terracing. Although the spaces in which flamenco is performed – initially inns and taverns, later cafés and theatres – are smaller, the point of contact with Greek theatre lies in the physical closeness of the spectators to the performing area and therefore in the feeling of intimacy which that proximity creates between performers and audience. The material of the Greek plays was, of course, extremely dark. Plays such as Aeschylus's *Agamemnon* and Sophocles's *Electra* and *Antigone* depicted events in which human beings experienced terrible suffering, were exposed to the most hideous of fates, and were seen to be, more often than not, the victims of implacable gods. Antigone, having defied Creon's decree that the body of her brother, Polynices, shall not be buried, is condemned to death; Creon's son, who is Antigone's betrothed, hangs himself in despair; Creon's wife, Eurydice, also commits suicide; and Creon himself is left, alone and despised, to contemplate the havoc he has wrought but which, in the end, the gods have engineered in order to take revenge upon his household. Although flamenco song does not deal with particular stories of this kind, the themes of implacable fate, human suffering, despair, unhappiness in love, and death, are all at its very heart, particularly in *cante grande*. Again, just as the stories of Greek tragedies would have been familiar to the audience prior to the performance of the play, so the flamenco singer's material, the themes and the words of the songs, represented in the past the experience of persecution and suffering shared by his listeners, and even now strikes a chord with anyone who has known misfortune or unhappiness in love.

In the Greek plays this process was defined by Aristotle as catharsis, which describes the purging of the powerful and conflicting emotions aroused in the audience by the drama. In flamenco, as we have seen, the singer both embodies the emotions of his listening audience in the sense that he is their voice, and releases them, often to such an extent that in a typical *juerga* many are reduced to weeping, tearing clothes and breaking chairs. This is, in effect, the cathartic reaction induced by Greek tragedy, pointing to the close parallel between that ancient form and flamenco.

Similarly, the relationship between flamenco and the bullfight may at first seem tenuous, but examination shows it to be surprisingly close. Consider the story *Carmen* in its various versions. In Prosper Mérimée's novella of 1845 the gypsy dancer becomes involved with the picador, Lucas, when she attends a bullfight in Córdoba. When Bizet composed his opera *Carmen*, first performed in 1875, his librettists transformed the rather ordinary picador into the much more glamorous bullfighter Escamillo and gave the bullfight itself considerable prominence in Act Four. More recently, in his film of 1983, the Spanish film director Carlos Saura retained the character of the bullfighter and also emphasized the relationship between the bullfight and flamenco. When in the film's final sequences Carmen flirts with the bullfighter, thereby arousing the jealousy of Antonio – Bizet's Don José – the two men challenge each other by performing in turn a short but expressive flamenco dance. There follows a characteristic flamenco song about love and jealousy passionately sung by the onlookers. Finally, when Antonio kills Carmen, his knife carries overtones of the bullfighter's sword, and the sand-coloured floor on which she lies is suggestive of the bull ring. Throughout the latter part of the film, Saura cleverly interweaves the threads of flamenco and the bullfight, thus expressing a connection deeply rooted in reality.

Many flamenco performers have been associated with bullfighting in one way or another, not least because both professions were in times past taken up

Carmen and the bullfighter, from the stage version by the Antonio Gades company

Two scenes from the
Gades *Carmen*:
confrontation of
Carmen's husband
and Don José;
Don José and Carmen

by gypsies. Aurelio Sellés, born in 1887 in Cádiz and of gypsy origin, considered bullfighting to be his first love and was, in fact, a *novillero* or apprentice bullfighter before he decided to dedicate himself to flamenco song. Juan Sánchez Valencia el Estampío, born around 1880 into a poor gypsy family from Jerez, tried his hand at bullfighting before he became a flamenco dancer. His movement in the dance was influenced in no small measure by his training as a bullfighter, and some of his dances were based on his experiences in the bull ring. The great Pastora Imperio was the daughter of a bullfighter's tailor and became the wife of Rafael Gallo, the bullfighter son of Fernando el Gallo, also a bullfighter, and the brother of Joselito, often considered to be the greatest bullfighter of all time. Fernando el Gallo's wife was the flamenco dancer Gabriela Ortega, and the family also counted among its members the singers El Planeta, Curro Dulce, Enrique Ortega, Carlota Ortega and Ignacio Espeleta. Related to them too was the great flamenco singer Manolo Caracol and, by marriage, the bullfighter Ignacio Sánchez Mejías, whose death in the ring in August 1934 would provide the inspiration for Lorca's famous poem, *Lament for Ignacio Sanchez Mejías*, with its strong flamenco resonance. Indeed, in many ways Sánchez Mejías perfectly illustrates the bullfight-flamenco connection, for, having retired from the bull ring prematurely in 1922, he turned

Lorca's torrero friend
Ignacio Sánchez
Mejías in Cádiz, 1930

163

to flamenco, as well as the theatre and literature. Although he came back to the bull ring, unable to resist its lure, his passion for flamenco continued. Though he was married, the great love of his life was the dancer Encarnación López Júlvez la Argentinita, with whom he helped to set up a company of Andalusian performers in 1931 and on whose behalf he also acted as impresario and talent-scout.

Another, deeper union between flamenco and the bullfight is to be found in their relationship to the ancient world. As we know, the region and city of Tartessus, now identified as south-west Andalusia, figured prominently in ancient history. But there also existed an earlier myth concerning the red cattle of King Geryon, which is the first link in the chain joining the ancient world with the modern bullfight. The tenth labour of Hercules was to capture the cattle of Geryon from Erytheia, an island near present-day Gilbraltar, and to do this he first journeyed to Tartessus. Arriving at Erytheia, Hercules succeeded in killing Geryon, seized the cattle and once again passed through Tartessus on the return journey to his homeland.

A second link between Andalusia, the bullfight and the ancient world concerns the worship of the Great Mother-Goddess, practised in former times throughout the Mediterranean. In some versions of the myth which underpinned this worship, the Mother-Goddess had a son or a husband who, in the form of an animal, frequently a bull, was sacrificed annually in order to assure the cycle of the seasons and the continuity of Nature. In Spain, the bull appears to have been venerated from pre-Roman times, and the ritual killing of bulls was common practice. Here, clearly, is the source of modern bullfighting in which the matador assumes the role of a priest as the bull is ritualistically slaughtered. There are present-day echoes of the myth of Geryon, for red cattle are still to be found in south-western Andalusia, and fighting bulls are also raised in the area.

For Lorca the bullfight represented the animate proof of an ancient civilization: '...the living spectacle of the ancient world in which are to be found the classical essences of the most artistic peoples in the world'. In describing a contemporary bullfighter, he attributed to him the smile of the historical king of Tartessus: 'Ignacio Espeleta... with a smile worthy of Arganthonius'. And in the lecture 'Play and Theory of the Duende', alluded to earlier in relation to flamenco, he concluded that the bullfight was not only supremely poetic but that, more than anything, it captured the vitality and passion of the classical world: '...bullfighting is probably the greatest poetic and vital wealth Spain possesses... It is as if all the "duende" of the classical world has come together in this perfect celebration...' The killing of the bull as part of a sacrificial rite therefore had its parallel in the modern bullfight which was, for Lorca, 'a religious mystery', while the bullfighter was the equivalent of the priest of ancient times: '... the cruel minister... his sword no less than the direct descendant of the sacrificial knife used by the priests of old...' Indeed, the religious connotations of this sacrifice, as well as its dramatic and even theatrical character, suggested to Lorca a clear similarity with the Catholic Mass, for if in the bullfight there is an echo of a sacrifice to a pagan god, so in the sacrament we are reminded of Christ's death so that mankind might be saved: 'the bullfight,

Goya's drawing of
a girl and a bull

Scene in the Barcelona
bull ring

a genuine religious drama in which, as in the Mass, a god is worshipped and sacrificed...'

The bullfighter, like the flamenco performer, is very much centre stage, the central player in a powerful drama. The drama in which he is engaged is, at its most basic, a confrontation between man and beast, between the rational and the irrational. The bull clearly embodies the instinctive and unpredictable power of Nature, its black colour a highly evocative pointer to the malevolence which, in the form of the bullfighter, man is required to face. In this respect the bull is the equivalent of those powerful forces with which, in the verses of flamenco song, particularly of *cante grande*, the individual is obliged to contend – forces which are suggested, for example, in the words of this *playera*:

Una noche e trueno One stormy night
yo pensé morí,   I thought I would die,
como tenía una   Because a black
  [sombra negra   *[shadow*
ensima de mí.   Hung over me.

Man alone against the bull; man alone confronted by fate. The struggle is essentially the same.

The contrast of light and shadow, an essential element in the bullfight, is highly suggestive. Because the spectacle takes place in the afternoon, normally beginning at 3 o'clock, part of the bull ring and part of the seating will be in sunlight, *sol*, and part in shadow, *sombra*. This has its practical implications, for the more expensive seats are in the shade, the cheapest in the sun, but the contrast has a metaphorical resonance too, for it echoes the clash of reason and unreason embodied in the arena in man and beast. As the flamenco singer embodies the life-struggle of his audience, so does the bullfighter personify and draw to himself the fluctuating moods of the crowd.

Bull ring scene in a miniature from a thirteenth-century Spanish manuscript

'Corrida', a rectangular
plate by Picasso, 1947

The appearance of the bull, large and dangerous, inevitably creates a shiver
of excitement, even of fear. Here, after all, is a dark, elemental force symbolic
of the adversity we all must face at some time in our lives. Each pass with the
cloak, as the bull comes close to the man, inspires a drawing of breath, a gasp
of apprehension. In the final stages, even though the bull is weakened, the
menace of that huge form still threatens as the bullfighter faces it alone, left to
his own devices. The final thrust of the sword, banishing all danger, releases
the crowd's pent-up emotions, producing a sense of relief which can fairly be
compared with the emotional effect described earlier in relation to both flamenco and Greek tragedy. The dark forces embodied in the bull are overcome
– even if the bullfighter is gored or killed, the bull will be despatched, the
threat averted, in ways they are not in flamenco song or Greek plays. But this
does not prevent us from acknowledging that flamenco and the bullfight are
embedded in the psyche of Andalusia in a deep and mysterious way.

Flamenco and the bullfight may also be compared in terms of their stylization and theatricality. In both flamenco song and dance, stylization is of the
essence, shaping the form of the song and the articulation of the dance. The
earlier account of the way Caracol performed a *siguiriya* reveals how words and
phrases are given special emphasis, repetitions are made, and pauses introduced to create dramatic effect. In other words, flamenco is carefully stylized,
structured by changes of pace and rhythm. In much the same way the bullfight

can be said to have its own distinctive structure, pace and rhythm. In *Death in the Afternoon* Ernest Hemingway draws attention to the dramatic nature and formal structure of the bullfight when he observes that it has three acts. The entry of the bullfighters and their assistants prior to the commencement of events is, in effect, the appearance of the actors on the stage before the performance begins. The first act involves the bullfighter's assistants, who use their capes to test which way the bull charges, and the mounted picadors who keep the bull at bay with a long lance, thrusting it into the tough muscle at the top of its neck. As in any good play, the first act sets the scene. In the second, the rhythm quickens. The *banderilleros*, or sometimes the bullfighter himself, run swiftly across the ring, deftly placing the *banderillas* – the yard-long sharp darts – two at a time in the back of the bull's neck. This is an episode of grace, fleet-footedness and beauty, comparable in its way to a dance. And then, of course, comes the final act, the most tense and dramatic of all, and this is itself composed of three sections. In the first the bullfighter dedicates the death of the bull to a particular individual; in the second he works the bull with the cloak in order to tire it and make it lower its head; and in the third he kills it by thrusting the sword between its shoulder blades. The three-act drama reaches its theatrical climax.

Action in the
Barcelona bull ring

Sketch of flamenco
performers by the
Spanish artist
Ricardo Canals

If the bullfight is essentially stylized, it is also spectacularly visual, and in that respect again similar to flamenco dance. Both can be justifiably compared in terms of colour and movement. Reds and blacks in particular stand out – black in the male dancer's waistcoat and trousers, as in the bull; red in the female's costume, as in the bullfighter's cloak. Indeed, in a mixed dance the male is frequently not unlike the bull – strong and aggressive – while the female, as graceful and quick as any bullfighter, keeps him at bay. In her swirling skirt there are echoes of the bullfighter's cape, in the male dancer's movement towards and around her echoes of the bull slipping by. In this respect it is revealing to recall the Ballet Rambert's dance-drama, *Cruel Garden*, first produced twenty years ago and recently revived. Based on the life and death of Lorca, it presents him as the bullfighter, the bull as the embodiment of malevolence, blind fury, prejudice and fate, and their confrontation presented in pure movement – dance and bullfight brilliantly combined.

The ultimate bond between flamenco and the bullfight – and it applies to religion too – is *duende*. In his lecture on this subject Lorca described it, as we have seen, as a magical, inspirational power, a Dionysian force, which drives the flamenco artist to produce an exceptional performance. But he also observed that 'duende is at his most impressive in the bullfight'. It is not enough for a bullfighter to be simply brave, for then he is merely putting his life at risk. In order to achieve a performance of true artistry, beauty, and invention, the bullfighter must be driven by that force which, as in the case of the flamenco performer, climbs up inside him 'from the soles of the feet', taking control of his very being. Such was the force which inspired the matadors Lagartijo, Belmonte, Joselito and Cagancho.

Flamenco, the bullfight, religion, all three closely interwoven, are in a sense the Holy Trinity of Spanish and, in particular, Andalusian cultural life. As we have seen, the points of contact between them are many and all three are deeply rooted in the region's psyche. Flamenco, in its early stages and for some time afterwards, remained a largely secretive and closed world, the domain of the gypsies and other disadvantaged groups in half a dozen towns and cities in south-west Spain. To a large extent it is an art form which is still distinguished by many of its ancient characteristics, even as it has spread its wings and made its mark far beyond its origins. Who can listen today to the singing of a *siguiriya* and hear the anguish of persecuted Andalusian gypsies several centuries ago? Who can watch the performance of a passionate flamenco dance and not sense that pride and defiance experienced by gypsy dancers in times past? To undergo such feelings now, in Madrid, London, New York or elsewhere, is to bear witness to the timeless values, the enduring appeal, and the universality of flamenco. However strange flamenco song may sound to uninitiated ears; however exotic flamenco dance appears to audiences unaccustomed to its flamboyance, the fact that flamenco touches chords within us points to the shared emotions and passions which it expresses – common human feelings evoked by all great art.

Flamenco, religion, bullfight: poster by José García Ramos for a programme of fiestas in Seville, 1907

EPILOGUE

Flamenco survives, but what of the gypsies themselves in present-day Spain? In the past, as we have seen, they were obliged by law to settle down and form communities, some of these no better than shanty towns, others more prosperous and respectable in the sense that those who settled there took up professions, as in the case of the blacksmiths and farriers of Triana. Even so, from the very outset the gypsies as a whole, considered to be outsiders, were regarded with suspicion and subjected to persecution, a circumstance that created the essentially dark mood of *cante jondo*. Those singers and dancers who performed it well became stars, and many of them moved out of their communities in order to enjoy a bigger stage. Others, in contrast, remained behind, preferring to practise their art in a familiar setting. The community, in short, was a constant factor, a source of belonging and of inspiration.

In recent times this situation has changed for a variety of reasons. For the last thirty years or so, many gypsies have abandoned their old communities in the hope of finding greater economic prosperity in the cities, in particular Madrid and Barcelona, and their children, though often steeped in flamenco traditions, have different concerns. The younger flamenco groups therefore reflect the way flamenco is now changing. Their music is strongly influenced by other traditions, such as rock, jazz and reggae, while the lyrics of their songs spring from a modern city background and the concerns of young people in the late 20th century. Even so, they seem to find it as difficult to integrate with their non-gypsy or '*payo*' neighbours as did their forefathers, and some of the old problems remain. In addition, many of the old gypsy communities where flamenco flourished have disappeared or been radically changed by modern urban development in the form of blocks of flats, and those people who have been forced to move inevitably feel a sense of resentment and injustice. In short, changed circumstances have had the effect of sustaining and even inflaming those feelings of persecution which originally underpinned flamenco. For that very reason, even though it is being affected by other musical forms, it seems unlikely that flamenco will disappear. Spain, despite its closer links with the rest of Europe, has always shown itself to be capable of preserving its great traditions.

Detail of the title-page on p.160

BIBLIOGRAPHY

Alvarez Caballero, Angel, *El cante flamenco*, Madrid 1994

Anderson, Andrew, *Lorca's Late Poetry*, Liverpool 1990

Barrios, Angel, *Gitanos, moriscos y cante flamenco*, Seville 1989

Borrow, George, *The Zincali: an Account of the Gypsies of Spain*, London 1907

Cadalso, José, *Cartas Marruecas*, Madrid 1963

Clébert, Paul, *The Gypsies* (tr. Charles Duff), New York 1963

Crichton, Ronald, *Falla*, London 1982

Demarquez, Suzanne, *Manuel de Falla* (tr. Salvator Attanasio), Philadelphia 1968

Estébanez Calderón, Serafín, *Escenas andaluzas*, Madrid 1960

Gades, Antonio and Saura, Carlos, *Carmen*, Barcelona 1984

García Lorca, Federico, *Gypsy Ballads* (tr. Robert Havard), Warminster 1990

Grande, Félix, *Memoria del flamenco*, Madrid 1979

Hemingway, Ernest, *Death in the Afternoon*, New York1932

Hernández, Mario, *Federico García Lorca: Poema del cante jondo*, Madrid 1994

Hooper, John, *The Spaniards: A Portrait of the New Spain*, Harmondsworth 1987

Hutton, Edward, *The Cities of Spain*, New York 1924

Kamen, Henry, *Spain 1469-1714: a Society in Conflict*, London 1983

Leblon, Bernard, 'La etapa secreta del cante', in *Dos siglos de flamenco*, Jerez 1989

Lee, Laurie, *A Rose for Winter*, London 1955

Machado y Alvarez, *Colección de cantes flamencos*, Madrid 1974

Antonio ('Demófilo') Maura, Christoper, *Federico García Lorca: Deep Song and Other Prose* (ed. and tr.), London 1980

Mitchell, Timothy, *Flamenco Deep Song*, New Haven 1994

Molina, Ricardo and Mairena, Antonio, *Mundo y formas del cante flamenco*, Madrid 1963

Morton, H.V., *A Stranger in Spain*, London 1955

Pohren, Donn, *The Art of Flamenco*, Madrid 1962

Lives and Legends of Flamenco, Madrid 1988

Quiñones, Fernando, 'Manolo Caracol, su vida, su arte', in *Blanco y Negro*, Madrid 1973

Sackville-West, Vita, *Pepita*, London 1937

Schreiner, Claus (ed.), *Flamenco*, Portland 1996

Tarby, Jean Paul, *Eros flamenco*, Cádiz 1991

Trend, J.B., 'A Festival in the South of Spain', in *Nation and the Athenaeum*, London, 8 July 1922

ACKNOWLEDGMENTS

Ken Haas's photographs are dedicated to two experts on Andalusia, one in the US and one in Spain, whose guidance and friendship were invaluable throughout the project:

DAVID D. GREGORY
JOSÉ ANTONIO VILORIA VALDÉS

Acknowledgment is due to the following individuals and institutions for kind assistance:

Paco Aguilera, Air Europa, Archivo Histórico Provincial, Granada (Eva Martín López), Ayuntamiento de Jerez, Promoción y Desarrollo de la Ciudad (Francisco Abuín Valle, Juan Martinez), María Susana Azzi, the late Mariano Baguena, Mr and Mrs José Cazorla Pérez, Centro Andaluz de Flamenco, Jerez (Calixto Sánchez Marín, Director), Pepe Chacón, Colorprint (Hong Kong), Costa del Sol Tourist Board (Antonio Andrade, Antonio Hernandez and D. Luis Vazquez), The Cristina Heeren Flamenco Foundation, Mr and Mrs Len Dunning, Enrique 'El Canastero' and colleagues Antonio Heredia, F. Rafaela Heredia and Nati Heredia, Epson, Fuji Photo Film USA, Debora Garber, Antonio Gonzalez ('El Cuqui'), Nancy G. Heller, Carlo Heredia and colleagues, José Heredia Maya and family, with special thanks to Pepe Heredia, Iberia Airlines, Larry Lavendar, Daniela Lazaro, Arturo Martínez, Meson El Chinitas Málaga (Sr José Sanchez Rosso, family and colleagues), Montoya Musical (Fernando Guerrero), Muséo Casa de los Tiros, Granada (Francisco Gonzalez de la Oliva, Director), PacRim Technologies (Hong Kong), Rafael Palmero Pérez, Patronato Provincial de Turismo de Granada (Manuel Múñoz Gutiérrez and M.ª Angustias Maldonado Cambil), Patronato Provincial de Turismo de Sevilla (Felisa Hernández Alonso), Peña Cultural Flamenca 'Torres Macarena' (Juan Heredia Vargas), Peña Manolo Caracol (Montalban), Javier Puga, Miguel Reyes and colleagues, Daryl Ries, José Antonio Santiago and family, Seville Bienal (Manuel Conradi, José Luis Ortiz Nuevo), Al and Diana Simonds, the late Robert Simpson, Henry Steiner, Francisco José Suarez-Barrera ('El Torombo'), Teatro Central Sevilla (Raquel Fuentes), Tivoli World, Benalmádena/Málaga (José Luis Guzmán García), Carmen and Juan de Torres Advincula, Maria del Carmen Viloria Valdés, William Washabaugh, Nathalie Wiegand, José Antonio Zamora Moya.

...and special thanks to the Tourist Office of Spain in New York.

SOURCES OF ILLUSTRATIONS

Bargello, Florence, 31 (*bottom*); Biblioteca Nacional, Madrid, 102; Bibliothèque Nationale, Paris, 19; British Library, London, 24 (*both*), 67 (*bottom*); Bodleian Library, Oxford, 30 (*left*); By courtesy of Angel Alvarez Caballero, 67 (*top*), 68, 69, 76 (*both*), 77, 115, 154; Castle Museum, Gaasbeck, Belgium, 21; Centro Andaluz de Flamenco, Jerez, 80; Dee Conway, London, 130 (*both*), 132, 136; Michel Dieuzaide, Toulouse, 26, 54, 55, 70 (*left*), 135 (*left*); El Escorial Library, 30 (*right*), 167; Manuel de Falla Archive, Granada, 159 (*centre*); Institut Amatler, Barcelona 73 (*both*); Isabella Stuart Gardner Museum, Boston, 70 (*right*); F.G. Lorca Foundation, Madrid, 78 (*both*), 160, 163; Andre Martin, 166, 169; Colette Masson/Agence Enguerand, Paris, 122 (*top*), 123 (*both*), 124, 126 (*both*) 128, 161, 162 (*right*); Museo Casa de los Tiros, Granada, 49, 65; Museo de Arte Moderna, Barcelona, 170; Museo del Prado, Madrid, 23, 165; Museo Nacional Centro de Arte Reina Sofia, 98; Museo Nazionale, Naples, 158 (*bottom*); Carlos Muñoz-Yague, 51, 116, 118, 19, 120, 129, 133, 135 (*right*); Palacio Real, Madrid, 155; Private Collection, 18, 28, 25 (*top*), 71, 72, 79, 100 (*bottom*), 103, 113 (*both*), 117, 171; Roger-Viollet, Paris, 66, 75, 99, 100 (*top*), 101; Ronald Grant Archive, London, 121, 125, 126

INDEX